The cost of this book
has been subsidized
by the
**RUTH HOME
MEMORIAL FUND**
established by the
members of the
Museums Section of
The Ontario Historical Society

The Loyal Americans

I never had an idea of subduing the Americans;
I meant to assist the good Americans subdue the
bad.

General James Robertson

The Loyal Americans

The Military Rôle of the Loyalist Provincial Corps
and Their Settlement in British North America, 1775–1784

Robert S. Allen, General Editor
Bernard Pothier, Coordinator of the Exhibition
Victor Suthren, Exhibition Designer

A travelling exhibition of the Canadian War Museum
in collaboration with the New Brunswick Museum

National Museum of Man/National Museums of Canada

© National Museums of Canada 1983

National Museum of Man
National Museums of Canada
Ottawa, Canada K1A 0M8

Catalogue No. NM 92–90/1983E

ISBN 0-660-10753-8

Édition française

Les loyalistes
Le rôle militaire des corps provinciaux loyalistes
et leur établissement en Amérique du Nord britan-
nique, 1775–1784

ISBN 0-660-90274-5

Printed and bound in Canada

Photographs

By Harry Foster, National Museum of Man, except
those on the following pages: p. 1, Delaware Art
Museum, Wilmington, Delaware; pp. 5, 67, 72, 78,
91, 101 (detail), 104 and 105 no. 155, Public Archives
of Canada, Ottawa (C-11242, C-11214, C-10548,
C-40162, C-95804, C-2001, C-2031 and C-2001 respec-
tively); p. 6, Canadian Conservation Institute, Ottawa;
p. 9, Canadian War Museum; p. 55, Patterson
Photographic, Ottawa; p. 18, National Museums of
Canada, Ottawa; pp. 22, 64 and 96, National
Gallery of Canada, Ottawa; p. 25, Musée du Québec,
Québec; p. 29, Toronto Historical Board, Toronto;
p. 39, Musée de l'île Sainte-Hélène, Montréal; p. 42,
George DeLancey Hanger, Roanoke, Virginia; pp. 61
and 109, Parks Canada, Ottawa; p. 81, New Brunswick
Museum, Saint John; p. 86 no. 131, Beaverbrook Art
Gallery, Fredericton; pp. 107 and 108, Royal Ontario
Museum, Toronto.

Coordination
Madeleine Choquette-Delvaux

Editor
Charis Wahl

Design
Acart Graphic Services Inc.

Printing
Alger Press

Contents

Foreword

Nineteen eighty-three marks the two-hundredth anniversary of the arrival of the Loyalists in the eastern provinces of present-day Canada. It is fitting that the Canadian War Museum mark this important bicentennial by commemorating the rôle of the Loyalist Provincial Corps during the civil war and rebellion in colonial America, and their subsequent establishment in what remained of British North America after the creation of the United States.

I am especially pleased to prepare a foreword for *The Loyal Americans*, for eight years ago I was actively associated with a closely related Canadian War Museum exhibition. It was entitled *Revolution Rejected, 1775-1776*, and commemorated the successful defence of Canada against the Americans at the start of the rebellion. On that occasion I contributed a volume to the Museum's Historical Publications Series and an introductory essay to the exhibition catalogue. In a sense, the present special exhibition marking the coming of the Loyalists beginning in 1775 completes the story begun by the Canadian War Museum in 1975. For, without an energetic defence in 1775 and 1776, Canada would not have provided a haven for the forty thousand Loyalists who settled here during and after the rebellion in the American colonies.

It therefore gives me great pleasure to offer my warmest wishes to Mr. Lee Murray, Chief Curator, and his staff for a very successful exhibition. It is a measure of the Canadian War Museum's accomplishment that, following its Ottawa sojourn, *The Loyal Americans* will first travel, significantly if ironically, to Lexington, Massachusetts, before continuing to Middleton, Nova Scotia, and Saint John, New Brunswick. By the end of its journey, this historic exhibition will have been seen in four regions of major and lasting Loyalist importance.

George F.G. Stanley
Lieutenant-Governor,
Province of New Brunswick

To the reader

The exhibition plans of several lenders have necessitated the withdrawal of a small number of works from some of the venues for *The Loyal Americans*. In the case of works of art, the organizers have substituted quality reproductions. Deletions and substitutions are so marked in the exhibition itself.

Introduction

The Loyal Americans: The Military Rôle of the Loyalist Provincial Corps and Their Settlement in British North America, 1775–1784 is a special exhibition assembled and organized by the Canadian War Museum to commemorate the contribution of the military Loyalists to Canada. The officers and men of the Loyalist Provincial Corps were for the most part born or long settled in North America. They were, therefore, truly ''American'' as the term was understood prior to the creation of the United States.

The British general, James Robertson, illustrated the contemporary meaning of ''American'' when he described his rôle in resisting the colonial rebellion. ''I never had an idea of subduing the Americans; I meant to assist the good Americans subdue the bad.'' The general's distinction so well illustrates the human context of the Thirteen Colonies during the rebellion that it has been chosen as an epigraph for both the catalogue and the title panel of the exhibition.

The Canadian War Museum's endeavour to commemorate the bicentennial of the coming of the Loyalists to Canada has been aided significantly by the cooperation of the New Brunswick Museum. At the inception of this project, David Ross, then the Director, offered us the pick of his institution's magnificent Loyalist collection. We amply profited from this kindness: fully twenty-two per cent of *The Loyal Americans* comes from the New Brunswick Museum.

In our efforts to represent military history prior to the nineteenth century, the Canadian War Museum depends significantly on the assistance of many institutions and private individuals in Canada, the United States, Great Britain, and continental Europe. The names of those who so generously contributed artefacts and works of art to *The Loyal Americans* are noted in the individual entries and are listed at the end of the catalogue.

In assembling *The Loyal Americans*, the general editor and the exhibition coordinator have closely communicated with curators in twenty-seven museums, galleries, and archives, as well as with sixteen private collectors. Both in our

personal capacities and on behalf of the Canadian War Museum we would like to express our gratitude for encouragement and cordiality to Dr. Ernst Aichner, Dr. Phyllis Blakeley, Harry Bosveld, Charles Bourque, Brenda Brownlee, James Burant, Eva Burnham, Darrel Butler, René Chartrand, Gaétan Chouinard, Dr. Brian Cuthbertson, Robert Elliot, Marie Elwood, Gregg Finley, Daniel Glennie, Conrad Graham, Paul Hachey, Elizabeth Hale, Dr. Wayne Hankey, Richard Harrington, James How, Joan Johnston, Betty Kidd, Alan McNairn, Joseph Martin, Pamela Miller, Dr. Helmut Nickel, Dr. Edward Rogers, Normand St-Pierre, Dr. Gisela Scheffler, Marilyn Smith, Judith Tomlin, Guy Vadeboncoeur, Donald Webster, Ronald Whate, and Norman Willis.

While pursuing field work and canvassing local historical societies and bicentennial committees, Loyalist descendants, and others in our quest for appropriate works, many individuals gave generously of their time and hospitality. To Mary Archibald, Rita Bower, Eileen and Judge Victor Cardoza, E.J. Chard, Mary and Donald Gillis, Dr. Wilfrid Johnston, Betty and John Wentworth Moody, and Warren Moore, we are particularly indebted.

As well, we owe much to our colleagues at the *Dictionary of Canadian Biography* and to several of that publication's contributors. Through Robert Fraser, Senior Manuscript Editor at the Dictionary, the following freely shared the fruits of their yet-unpublished biographical research: Peter Browne, Robert Burns, William Godfrey, Barbara Greymont, Reginald Horsman, Stanley Mealing, and Stuart Sutherland.

We wish to express our thanks to the Loyalist scholars who, with the general editor, have contributed introductory essays to the chapters of this catalogue: Dr. Phyllis Blakeley, Professors Wallace Brown, Ann Gorman Condon, and George A. Rawlyk. We are also grateful to several of our own colleagues in both the Canadian War Museum and the National Museum of Man. One too often takes for granted the indispensable collaboration of editors, designers, photographers, managers, typists, and exhibit preparators. Clarence Adams, Jacqueline Cléroux, Madeleine Choquette-Delvaux, Frank

Corcoran, Alan Fell, Harry Foster, James MacLeod, Lee Murray, Victor Suthren, Dr. William Taylor, Jr., and Charis Wahl all contributed their particular skills to this endeavour.

Finally, we very much appreciate the support of the Treaties and Historical Research Centre of the Department of Indian and Northern Affairs. Thanks to the generosity of the Centre, the general editor has been able to participate in field trips and editorial meetings, and generally to attend to many developmental details over some eighteen months.

The impact of the arrival and settlement of the Loyalist refugees in Canada during late 1783 and 1784 was unique, profound, and permanent. There were close to forty thousand men, women, and children who had suffered hardship and humiliation, endured a long, bitter war, and undergone immense material sacrifices in their attempt to preserve and defend the unity of the empire.

The Loyalist contribution was not the same in every province of British North America. About twenty thousand Loyalists settled in peninsular Nova Scotia, a province already heavily settled by various ethnic and religious groups. There, the Loyalist settlers eventually came to share in what was already a fully constituted province. About fourteen thousand refugees came to New Brunswick. Although Malecite (Maliseet) people and some hundreds of Acadian families were already there, it is known to this day as the Loyalist province. Smaller groups of Loyalists settled in Newfoundland, St. John's (Prince Edward) Island, and Cape Breton Island.

About six thousand Loyalists sought refuge in the "old" Province of Quebec. While some remained in the established parts of the province, most trekked to the unoccupied western portions, which Governor Haldimand had opened to settlement. This region subsequently became Upper Canada (Ontario). Unlike New Brunswick, this new province of British North America saw the influence of the Loyalists

tempered by the arrival of thousands of post- or late-Loyalists. These came from the United States, partly as a result of disillusionment with the new republic.

Throughout British North America, the Loyalists contributed to the fashioning of a distinct and markedly different nation from the one they had been forced to flee. Their arrival and settlement produced an evolving federal concept based on the principle of two founding peoples; for the Loyalists and the French-Canadians formed the warp and weft of the fundamental political and cultural fabric of Canadian life.

This is less apparent today than it was a hundred years ago. The Loyalist mystique is no longer as strong socially or politically as it once was. Indeed, one might well question how much of the Loyalist heritage endures in Canada. Nevertheless, it is of real and lasting significance. In central Canada the Loyalists introduced such British political institutions as representative government, a constitutional cornerstone. In Atlantic Canada, parliamentary democracy based on a constitutional monarchy entrenched its British character. In Quebec, these political institutions proved both the inspiration and a powerful instrument for the achievement of "survivance" for the Francophone population. These contributions will ensure that the Loyalists will always remain an integral part of Canada's national heritage.

Robert S. Allen
Deputy Chief,
Treaties and Historical Research Centre,
Department of Indian and Northern Affairs
General Editor

Bernard Pothier
Curator of Historical Resources,
Canadian War Museum
Exhibition Co-ordinator

The Foundations of Loyalism
by Ann Gorman Condon

Associate Professor of History
University of New Brunswick at Saint John

Loyalty, any statesman would agree, is the finest gift a citizen can offer to his community. In times of revolution or civil war, however, one man's loyalty becomes another's treason. During the American Revolution, some men and women believed that it was their duty to take up arms, dissolve their ties with Great Britain, and establish a new nation in North America. Other Americans, equally committed to the welfare of their homeland, fought to preserve the unity of the British Empire in America, to maintain the rule of law and to support its embodiment, King George III. While the Patriots wrote the Declaration of Independence, marched with George Washington to victory and established the American republic, the Loyalists fought with pen and musket in all Thirteen Colonies, marched side-by-side with the British regulars until their world was turned upside down at Yorktown, and then retreated into privacy or exile with the defeat of their cause. The great irony of the American Revolution is that both the Loyalists and the Patriots believed that they were fighting to preserve American liberty.

An understanding of the Loyalists' special vision of the future of North America and their distinctive definition of liberty is as necessary to an understanding of Canadian history as of American history. After the war, forty thousand Loyalist exiles resettled in Nova Scotia and created two new provinces—New Brunswick and Upper Canada (Ontario). They built new homes and new communities, and established an elaborate set of governments, churches, universities, schools, landholding systems, and social rituals that drew on their experience in colonial America. The new American republic and the fledgling colonies of British North America were the offspring of the same political upheaval, and the Loyalist experience illuminates the cultural similarities and differences of these two societies.

Who were these other Americans, these men and women who called themselves "the suffering Loyalists"? British General James Robertson hailed them as "the good Americans".[1] American General George Washington denounced them as "Unhappy wretches! Deluded mortals!"[2] A rebel jibe defamed the Loyalist as "a thing whose head is in England, and its body in America, and [whose] neck ought to be stretched".[3] Such vivid name-calling was the product of wartime passions. But long after the

war had ended, the Loyalists continued to be misunderstood and misrepresented. Until very recent times, British historians have generally ignored the Loyalists. American historians have been inclined to dismiss them as weak and unimaginative hangers-on, as lackeys of the Crown. To dispel this image, many descendants of the Loyalists and such devout groups as the United Empire Loyalists' Association of Canada have written histories depicting their ancestors as the personification of honour, courage, and self-sacrifice.

There emerge from these early, zealous accounts two stereotypes of the Loyalists. According to one, the Loyalists were an élite band of colonial aristocrats—courageous, swashbuckling figures of distinguished lineage. They attended Harvard College and then devoted themselves to managing their vast estates, serving the public, and raising noble families. When a vulgar mob unjustly rebelled against their King, they were forced to take up arms and fight the rebels with such ferocity that after their defeat they had to retreat to Canada, England, or the British West Indies as exiles.

According to the second early stereotype, the Loyalists were humble farmers, frontiersmen, Blacks, Indians, urban labourers, and immigrants. These "folk Loyalists" were too hard-pressed and untaught to comprehend the larger political issues, but they possessed a childlike devotion to their King, as their actions during and after the Revolution vividly demonstrated.

These two stereotypes, which dominated Loyalist history and mythology for almost two centuries, do not entirely misrepresent the Loyalist movement, but they do oversimplify it. Recent historians have discovered beneath these superficial images a more complex, diverse and philosophically profound movement than the earlier "heroic" histories suggest. Historians now estimate that approximately half a million people—about twenty per cent of the American population of 1776—became Loyalists.[4] Their research also suggests that the Loyalists were a heterogeneous group, with every colony and practically every segment of American society represented in the ranks.

This great Loyalist mass can be divided into three categories.

Those who fall in the first category became Loyalists because they had a vested interest in the imperial establishment. They included colonial governors, royal officials, judges, and

Anglican ministers preaching in areas, such as the Middle Colonies and New England, where the followers of the King's faith were a minority. An equally obvious interest motivated merchants who traded with English or Scottish firms, and some lawyers who had been trained in the English Inns of Court and felt tied to the established order.

Another kind of vested interest was shown by certain partisans who joined the Loyalist ranks not out of commitment to the empire but because of their political stand on local issues. The Carolina Regulators, the Pennsylvania merchants and some of the New York tenantry, for example, were primarily concerned with such local issues as the organization of county government, frontier defence, and land tenure, and they saw Loyalism as a means of gaining their political objectives.

As in most wars, the great majority of people in the American Revolution did not want to get involved. Their only interest was in survival. Nevertheless, they were drawn in—some as Loyalists, some as rebels—because of the disposition of the opposing armies, partisan pressure or simply fear. The diversity of the groups in this first category demonstrates that a great host of people became Loyalists for reasons quite unrelated to British imperial policy or to the issue of American independence.

Loyalists in the second general category displayed more subtle motives. They were members of religious and cultural minorities who had not joined mainstream American colonial society, and who clung to British protection out of fear of increased American power. Some were religious groups with idiosyncratic beliefs: French Huguenots, Maryland Catholics, and Quaker pacifists. Many were recent immigrants from Germany, Holland or the British Isles. Finally, there were those two ostracized minorities—the Native people and the Black slaves. Traditionally, the Indian tribes had recognized that the officers of the British Indian Department were the only barrier between them and American frontiersmen and unscrupulous colonial land speculators. In some of the most ferocious fighting of the war, the Indian tribes gave their formidable support to the British army. Black support, on the other hand, was less than expected. Although the British made extensive efforts to lure slaves away from their rebel masters by promising them freedom and land, the results were disappointing. Most of the slaves, systematically denied experience in decision-making, were simply unable to respond to such a call.

The loyal men and women who belonged to these religious and cultural minorities did not draw up fine documents or make grand speeches. However, they did show remarkable insight into one tendency of Revolutionary politics. All of them felt that their political position and personal beliefs were safer under British rule than under the newly proclaimed American government. As outsiders, they perceived the conforming impulse in American politics—the tendency of a committee or a mob or the Sons of Liberty to impose their views on everyone, the tendency which Alexis de Tocqueville would later describe as ''the tyranny of the majority''.[5] It is significant that these aliens and non-conformists chose British tolerance over the much more trumpeted American ideal of liberty.

Loyalists of the third and most famous category were the Tory élite, the group of colonial leaders who opposed the Revolution out of principle, who wrote the pamphlets, proposed the plans, led the regiments during the war, and then retired to England or embraced new colonial challenges elsewhere. A roll call of their names—Hutchinson, Oliver, Winslow, Sewell, Robinson, DeLancey, Fairfax, Johnson, Skinner, Galloway, Odell, Franklin, Chipman, Bayard, Coffin, Phillipse—encompasses a long and impressive record of service to the colonies in peace and war, and in the service of God.

By any standard they were impressive men. Most had been born in the colonies and many of their families had lived there for two or more generations. Many attended college or trained for a profession. They were ''gentlemen'' in the eighteenth-century, deferential sense of that word—men trained to manage large estates or enterprises, lead troops, preach the gospel or bear public responsibility. These cultivated, seasoned leaders were thoroughly at home in the political and social worlds of both London and colonial America. Unlike the other Loyalists, they were not bound to the empire by vested interests or a sense of dependency. On the contrary, they were courted assiduously by the Revolutionary leaders to join their movement. The decision of the élite to oppose American independence was a matter of careful reflection and free choice based on a vision of the future and a concern for liberty.

Like virtually all colonial Americans, the élite

had an optimistic, expansive vision of the future of North America. The extraordinary resources of the continent and its young, enterprising population clearly held the promise of prosperity and world power. The Loyalist élite wished to tap this rich potential by means of an Anglo-American empire—a joint partnership that would link the wealth, cultural richness, and military strength of Great Britain to the resources and energies of North America. These Tory leaders believed that the colonies should be granted internal self-government, but they maintained that this could be achieved without abandoning the strength, stability, and enlightenment that the British connection provided.

Like the Revolutionary leaders, the Tory élite opposed the taxation system and administrative restrictions that Britain imposed on the colonies in the 1760s, and they made their protests heard in London. However, these highly sophisticated members of colonial society were even more dismayed by the newness and apparent crudeness of American life. Colonial America had just emerged from primitive frontier conditions. Its institutions were immature, its leadership poorly trained, its social relations still threatened by anarchy and brutality. The civil upheavals and riots preceding the Revolution, which had caused wanton destruction of property, tarring and feathering, persecution of beliefs, and other violations of liberty, convinced many colonial leaders that the greatest threat to freedom in America came not from the King but from the mob. As Reverend Mather Byles put it: "Which is better—to be ruled by one tyrant three thousand miles away or three thousand tyrants not a mile away?"[6] Fearing what Jonathan Sewell termed "the intoxicating charm of the word liberty",[7] the élite supported the continuation of British rule in America believing that it would produce a way of life that was richer—and freer—than any the colonists could provide for themselves.

Loyalist opposition to the Revolutionary movement meant that the rebellion was a civil war as well as a war for independence. In some areas, notably New York and the Carolinas, the struggle between the factions for local power was more important than imperial concerns. The personal toll was high: the loss of lives, families, fortunes and hopes, and the loss to colonial America of almost eighty thousand valuable citizens.

It is important for us to recall the Loyalists, to take note of their circumstances and their ideals, to admire their courage and to acknowledge their shortcomings. But it is more important for citizens of a democratic society to consider afresh the powerful critique that Loyalist history provides of the forces unleashed by revolution.

A.G.C.

1. See W. Brown, *The Good Americans* (Toronto and New York, 1969), p. vi.
2. C.S. Crary, ed., *The Price of Loyalty: Tory Writings from the Revolutionary Era* (New York, 1973), p. 7.
3. Brown, *Good Americans*, p. 226.
4. P.H. Smith, "The American Loyalists: Notes on their Organization and Numerical Strength," *William and Mary Quarterly*, no. 25 (1968), pp. 259–77.
5. A. de Toqueville, *Democracy in America* (New York, 1961), vol. 1, p. 304.
6. Brown, *Good Americans*, p. 74.
7. A. Condon, "Marching to a Different Drummer: The Political Philosophy of the American Loyalists," in E.C. Wright, ed., *Red, White & True Blue* (New York, 1976), p. 11.

1. George III, King of Great Britain
Richard Houston, after a painting by Jeremiah Meyer
English
3rd quarter, 18th century
Mezzotint engraving
31.8 cm × 24.8 cm

Picture Division, Public Archives of Canada, Ottawa
No. C-11242

The reign of George III (1738–1820) was plagued in the early years by a succession of weak and divided ministries at a time when Great Britain required strong and united leadership. By the early 1770s many American colonists had come to believe that England was facing a new despotism, reminiscent of the reign of Charles I (1625–1649). However, it is likely that most feeling was vented against the King's advisors, who were perceived to be wicked, conspiring men, even by future Loyalists.

George III, as commander of the British Army, took a direct interest in the conduct of the American war and proved skilful in gaining the cooperation of his Parliament.

2. Proclamation for Suppressing Rebellion and Sedition
1775
Reproduction, original in the New York Public Library, New York

By permission of the New York Public Library, New York

The King's proclamation for suppressing rebellion and sedition, issued in August 1775, was received with hisses in London. For even in England the American war was not popular in all quarters. Opposition both in and outside Parliament gathered strength as the rebellion continued, though the nation generally favoured ministerial policy.

3. Red Ensign
British
Ca. 1783
Wool
256.0 cm × 142.0 cm

Canadian War Museum, Ottawa
No. 1981-296/93

This red ensign bears the first Union Jack, proclaimed in 1707. The cross of St. Patrick did not appear as part of the Union Jack until 1801. The provenance of this historic ensign can be traced back to the loyal Ottawa Indians of the old Northwest, who in all probability acquired it either during or shortly after the rebellion.

Born in Ireland, William Johnson (1715–1774) came to the Mohawk Valley of upper New York province in 1738 as an agent for his uncle, Peter Warren. Within a decade of his arrival he became influential, involved in trade, land transactions, and Indian affairs. In 1756 he was appointed colonel of the Iroquois Confederacy of Six Nations.

Johnson was of great value to the British government. For his part in the defeat of a strong French column under Jean-Armand Dieskau at Lake George (Lac Saint-Sacrement) in 1755, he received a baronetcy, and in the following year he was appointed superintendent of Indian affairs for the northern district. Johnson's influence continued after the fall of New France. He was instrumental in the conduct of Indian affairs, and was a key figure in negotiating Indian land surrender, notably of

the Treaty of Fort Stanwix in 1768. However, Johnson was not immune to personal land speculation at the Indians' expense. Indeed, it has been claimed that he was one of their principal exploiters. He was distinguished from others of his ilk, however, by "the great advantages he possessed through his office and through his long intimacy with the Indians".

At a large Six Nations Conference in July 1774 Johnson made a successful four-hour speech imploring the Iroquois to remain neutral in Lord Dunmore's War. He then collapsed and died. To the end he remained a loyal servant of the King.

4. Sir William Johnson
Francisco Bartolozzi
British
3rd quarter, 18th century
Stipple engraving and etching
8.9 cm × 7.2 cm

McCord Museum, Montreal
No. M-6125

Note: Uniform detail and coiffure suggest that, despite its title, this work probably portrays Sir William's son John. Compare with item no. 19.

5. Sir William Johnson in counsel with the Iroquois at Johnson Hall, Mohawk Valley, Upper New York, 1774
Photographic reproduction of a painting by Edward Lamson Henry

By permission of Mr. John B. Knox, Lake Pleasant, New York

6. Indian medal
British
Eighteenth century
Silver
Obverse, Bust of George III
Diam. 7.7 cm

National Medal Collection, Public Archives of Canada, Ottawa
No. 1617

7. Indian medal
British
Eighteenth century
Silver
Reverse, Royal Arms
Diam. 7.7 cm

National Medal Collection,
Public Archives of Canada,
Ottawa
No. 1615

The Loyalist Provincial Corps
by Robert S. Allen

Deputy Chief, Treaties and Historical Research Centre
Department of Indian and Northern Affairs, Ottawa

The "shots heard 'round the world" at Lexington and Concord in April 1775 initiated not only a rebellion in colonial America but also a cruel and bitter civil war. From the commencement of hostilities, colonial Americans fought each other in an internecine rivalry that became increasingly shocking and bloody. The loyal Americans, those men and women who supported the royal cause, did so for a variety of reasons. Faced with a difficult decision, some merely followed what they had been taught to believe as children—to "Fear God and Honour the King".[1] Many more genuinely believed in the superiority of British political institutions and in the wisdom of preserving the unity of the empire. Others were persuaded to follow prominent, influential or charismatic Loyalist leaders, like Sir John Johnson in the Mohawk valley of upper New York, Oliver DeLancey of Long Island, Cortlandt Skinner of New Jersey or David Fanning of North Carolina.

These Loyalists organized themselves into bodies of irregulars, independent companies, loyal militia, and, most significantly, into uniformed, fully armed, and accoutred Loyalist provincial corps. Initially raised for local defence only, the exigencies of war soon necessitated the use of the provincial corps in areas far from home, and thus they served throughout the Thirteen Colonies, and in Nova Scotia, Newfoundland, Prince Edward Island, and in the province of Québec. Loyalist troops were stationed in Bermuda and the British West Indies, especially in Jamaica and the Bahamas.[2] They were also active in Central America, most notably in the successful raid of the Loyal American Rangers against the Spanish post at Black River, Honduras. Other loyal Americans joined the Royal Navy and the batteaux service or engaged in privateering.

In spite of the Loyalist enthusiasm for the royal cause, the British did not exert themselves at the beginning of the conflict to gain the sympathy and support of the loyal population of colonial America. British strategists were convinced that the rebellion could be suppressed quickly and efficiently solely through the use of British regulars assisted by hired troops from several German states. This, however, proved to be a serious military miscalculation. British and German troops were steady and competent in open fields, but fighting in the hills, woods, and swamps of colonial America against an elusive and unorthodox enemy was a difficult undertaking.

Moreover, the royal forces soon realized that in order to defeat the colonial rebels, they had to venture into the interior. The Royal Navy controlled the seas, and the British could establish operational bases along the coastline, which could be supplied by ships from home. However, the logistical problems became a nightmare each time the forces attempted to march inland, as lines of communications became vulnerable to constant harassment. These difficulties, asserted a senior British officer, "absolutely prevented us this whole war from going fifteen miles from a navigable river".[3]

The British had become painfully aware that "the assistance of the Loyal Inhabitants is essential to the success of all operations within land".[4] In spite of the contention of one Loyalist officer from South Carolina that "almost every British officer regarded with contempt and indifference the establishment of a militia among a people differing so much in custom and manners from themselves",[5] British military policy was revised to assist "the good Americans to subdue the bad". At first largely ignored and then relied upon too heavily, especially in the colonial South after 1778, the loyal Americans became crucial for controlling the country and achieving a royal victory.

Notwithstanding the early British attitude towards Loyalists-in-arms, some provincial corps were organized soon after Lexington and Concord. Most of the corps, however, were not formed until the latter part of 1776 or 1777. A few units, such as the Duke of Cumberland's Regiment (also known as Montagu's), the King's American Dragoons, and the small contingent of loyal Blacks known as the British Negro Horse, were not raised until near the end of the conflict.

Most of the corps had an affiliation or association with a particular province, which was reflected in the corps' name, but this does not mean that the rank and file of a specific corps were drawn from that area or province. In Massachusetts during the spring of 1775, for example, Timothy Ruggles of Boston raised the Loyal American Association, a unit that wore no uniform, but was identified by a white sash worn on the left arm.[6] Thomas Gilbert of Bristol County, who "was known for his loyalty to his King", gathered three hundred loyal Americans for local defence.[7] The Loyal Irish

Volunteers, Wentworth's Volunteers, and the Company of Negroes served at the siege of Boston. All these units were understrength, short-lived and eventually merged with other Loyalist provincial corps. In New Hampshire, Connecticut, and Rhode Island, no Loyalist provincial corps was formed, but numerous individuals from these provinces enlisted. Many New Englanders filled the ranks of the Queen's Rangers, the King's American Regiment, and the Prince of Wales American Regiment.

Three major Loyalist provincial corps raised in 1775 were associated with Nova Scotia. Following royal approval to raise corps of "His Majesty's Loyal North American Subjects" for the defence of Nova Scotia and Québec, Lieutenant Colonel Allan Maclean recruited veteran Highlanders who had settled in Nova Scotia, Québec, New York, and North Carolina. He and his officers also recruited recent emigrants to form the Royal Highland Emigrants. The second of its two battalions served under Major John Small in Nova Scotia. In 1779 the corps was placed on the British regular establishment as The 84th Regiment of Foot (Royal Highland Emigrants). Lieutenant Colonel Joseph Goreham was also issued "beating orders" and organized the Royal Fencible Americans. Governor of Nova Scotia Francis Legge, responding to the pleas to form "an Association to defend his Majesty's Crown and dignity and the authority of Great Britain against all opposers", raised and commanded a third corps, the Loyal Nova Scotia Volunteers (designated Royal after 1780). In addition, three small units, Timothy Hierlihy's Corps, the St. John's Volunteers, and a part of the King's Rangers, served in the defence of Nova Scotia and Prince Edward Island. A number of men from the Royal Fencible Americans transferred or re-enlisted into the new Royal Newfoundland Regiment. This provincial corps, under the command of Major Robert Pringle, was known as Pringle's Foot and garrisoned St. John's from 1780 to 1783.[8]

Several Loyalist provincial corps served in the province of Québec. The 1st Battalion of the Royal Highland Emigrants under Allan Maclean contributed significantly to the successful military defence of the province, particularly during the siege of Québec in 1775 and 1776. The corps subsequently provided solid garrison strength at Québec, Montréal, Carleton Island, Niagara, and even at the distant fur trade and military post of Michilimackinac in the upper Great Lakes.[9] Sir John Johnson, son and heir to the massive estates of Sir William Johnson, raised two battalions of the King's Royal Regiment of New York, called the Royal Yorkers. The 1st Battalion, formed at Montreal in 1776, was composed mainly of Scotch Highlanders and other tenants from Sir John's estates in the Mohawk Valley. The 2nd Battalion was formed in 1780.[10]

Butler's Rangers, also recruited largely of men from the Mohawk Valley, was organized in 1777 by Major, later Lieutenant Colonel, John Butler. This corps was particularly active and daring in conducting raids against rebel back settlements in New York and Pennsylvania. Directly linked with Butler's Rangers were the Loyalist officers of the British Indian Department, men like Matthew Elliott and Simon Girty, and His Majesty's Indian Allies, especially the Mohawk Loyalists of the Iroquois Confederacy of Six Nations led by Joseph Brant, John Deserontyon, and Aaron Hill.[11] The King's Rangers, under the command of Major James Rogers, garrisoned Saint-Jean and other posts along the Richelieu River. The King's Loyal Americans and the Queen's Loyal Rangers, together with a number of independent companies, were reorganized in November 1781 to form the Loyal Rangers (Jessup's Corps).[12]

The royal province of New York remained a British and Loyalist stronghold throughout the war, and numerous Loyalist corps were affiliated with the province. The New York Volunteers, according to their commander Lieutenant Colonel George Turnbull, were "imbodied so Early as 1775 that we had a Share in the Dangers of the Actions of 27th August 1776 on Long Island".[13] Indeed, although the Volunteers consisted of only two companies in the summer of 1776, they landed with the British army from Halifax; and with only the wretched remnant of the apparel in which they had escaped from the rebels six or eight months before, they eagerly engaged the enemy and took part in the royal victories of that year. The corps was soon strengthened and properly uniformed, and campaigned actively for the duration of the war.

The Westchester Loyalists supplied forage and provisions for the garrison in New York. The largest Loyalist provincial corps in New York was the three battalions of DeLancey's Brigade, commanded by Brigadier General Oliver DeLancey, raised initially "for the defence of Long Island and other exigencies". Other New

York corps of military significance included Queen's Rangers, King's Orange Rangers, King's American Regiment, Loyal American Regiment and their affiliate the Guides and Pioneers, Prince of Wales American Regiment, British Legion, American Volunteers, Emmerich's Chasseurs, First Independent Company of New York Rangers, Royal Garrison Battalion (elements of which were stationed in Bermuda), American Legion, and, to a lesser extent, the King's American Dragoons.

Other provinces formed and organized Loyalists-in-arms in a similar manner. The largest single Loyalist provincial corps was the New Jersey Volunteers, which eventually consisted of six battalions. Raised by Brigadier General Cortlandt Skinner in 1776, the corps was involved for a time in plundering the surrounding countryside for forage and cattle, and thus was dubbed "Skinner's Cowboys".[14] Some battalions of the corps subsequently campaigned in the colonial South.

The Pennsylvania Loyalists and the Maryland Loyalists were combined into the United Provincial Corps of Pennsylvania and Maryland Loyalists in 1779. The corps was despatched to defend Pensacola in West Florida, but after a long and costly siege they surrendered to Spanish forces in May 1781. Pennsylvania was also represented by the Volunteers of Ireland, Bucks County Dragoons, Philadelphia Light Dragoons, Caledonian Volunteers and the Black Company of Pioneers. The dragoons and volunteers became part of the British Legion.

In Virginia two short-lived units were assembled: the Queen's Own Loyal Virginia Regiment, which soon formed a significant part of the Queen's Rangers, and the Ethiopian Regiment, an ex-slaves unit of loyal Blacks. The Royal North Carolina Regiment, North Carolina Highlanders (Volunteers), South Carolina Royalists and Dragoons, Georgia Loyalists and Light Dragoons, East Florida Rangers, and King's (Carolina) Rangers were some of the other major Loyalist provincial corps that made important contributions to the military efforts of His Majesty's Government during the colonial rebellion.

In order to raise Loyalist provincial corps quickly and to encourage recruitment, the British government provided various incentives. Influential and preferably wealthy loyal Americans were granted warrants to organize and command military regiments. As well, in-dividuals were awarded commissions if they were able to muster sufficient men for a platoon, company or battalion. The officer classification ultimately depended upon the number of recruits collected by the individual. Recruits, who were to serve two years or "during the present war in North America", received a bounty of money upon enlistment and the promise of a land grant following the end of hostilities. Finally, through the creation of the American establishment, five Loyalist provincial corps were placed on an equal level with British regular regiments. The corps so honoured were, in order, the Queen's Rangers, designated and numbered by His Majesty as The 1st American Regiment (2 May 1779), followed by the Volunteers of Ireland, the New York Volunteers, the King's American Regiment, and the British Legion.[15] All these corps had particularly distinguished war-service records.

Each Loyalist provincial corps was provided with uniforms and accoutrements, and was armed with the older Long Land tower musket or "Brown Bess". Although the provincials traditionally wore green, the British decided in about 1778 that red would give them a more professional bearing. By the end of the war, most of the Loyalist corps were uniformed in red faced with blue, green, orange, buff or other colour facings. A few corps, however, such as the Queen's Rangers, British Legion and Butler's Rangers, refused to alter their uniforms and retained their distinctive field green. By the last year of the rebellion, there were about fifty provincial corps, totalling nearly ten thousand Loyalists.

British authorities early in the war organized four military departments in vital areas where the royal forces were dominant. The eastern or northeastern was Nova Scotia, the northern, the province of Québec, the central, the city of New York and environs, and the southern, East Florida. In all four theatres, Loyalist provincial corps served with efficiency and courage.

Nova Scotia was not a major military front in the colonial rebellion. The Royal Navy along the seabound coast ensured the King's order in the province. However, at Fort Cumberland on the Isthmus of Chignecto in November 1776, the Royal Fencible Americans thwarted the Eddy rebellion, an incursion bolstered by a few "deluded" locals. To preserve the hinterland of the province and defend against further enemy aggression, Fort Howe, at the mouth of the St.

John River, was built and garrisoned by the fencibles in the late autumn of 1777. Halifax and area remained secure throughout the war; nonetheless, the defences were strengthened by garrison troops from the Royal Highland Emigrants and Loyal Nova Scotia Volunteers. Fort Edward at Windsor was also manned by Loyalist troops.

The successful military defence of Nova Scotia during the rebellion was marred only by the sea raids of American rebel privateers against the people and towns of the province and adjacent areas. As early as November 1775 marauders raided Charlottetown, plundering its stores and houses. Similar "wanton depredations" were committed at St. Peter's and Georgetown (Saint John's, now Prince Edward Island).

Prince Edward Island defences, however, were slowly strengthened by the increasing military presence of the St. John's Volunteers, Hierlihy's Corps, and the King's Rangers. Other areas were similarly protected, especially the coastal towns along the south shore of Nova Scotia, which were particularly vulnerable. Liverpool, for example, received a detachment of the King's Orange Rangers in December 1778 to assist the local militia. Although Nova Scotia was never seriously threatened, not all areas were immune from attack. In late August 1781, American privateers captured the blockhouse and sacked the town of Annapolis Royal.[16]

The province of Québec was nearly captured by the colonial rebels in the winter of 1775–1776. Chambly, Saint-Jean, and Montréal had fallen. But the enemy attack against the town of Québec, during a blinding snowstorm on the night of 31 December 1775, was crushed. Preeminent in this successful defence were Allan Maclean and the Royal Highland Emigrants. The siege of Québec was lifted the following spring with the arrival of the Royal Navy and reinforcements. Thereafter, the province became a base for the Burgoyne and St. Leger expeditions of 1777 and subsequent Loyalist raids. Some of the most intense fighting of the war took place on this northern front. At Oriskany in the Mohawk Valley, the civil-war nature of the conflict was never more starkly brutal as American Loyalists, mostly Royal Yorkers, grappled with American rebels in bitter hand-to-hand fighting on 6 August 1777. Only a heavy rain and physical exhaustion finally forced the ex-neighbours to cease. At Bennington the Queen's Loyal Rangers were nearly annihilated by colonial Americans on 16 August 1777.

In 1778 Butler's Rangers and their Iroquois allies, based at Niagara, wreaked havoc on enemy settlements at Wyoming Valley, German Flats, and Cherry Valley. The following year, the rebels mounted the Sullivan expedition in retaliation, and although the ancient villages of the Mohawk Loyalists and other Iroquois of the Six Nations Confederacy were destroyed, Fort Niagara was preserved. Sir John Johnson and his Royal Yorkers led two major raids into the Mohawk Valley in May and October 1780. The following autumn Loyalist troops attacked the valley again. Even as late as the summer of 1782, Butler's Rangers and His Majesty's Indian allies were continuing the fight. They won two successive and decisive victories against the colonial rebels, in June at Sandusky and in August at Blue Licks, where the legendary Daniel Boone was among the routed. By 1783 the British, Loyalists, and Indian allies were still firmly in possession of the province of Québec and the western posts. In spite of the terms of the peace, Niagara, Detroit, Michilimackinac, and other places would not be relinquished to the new republic for another thirteen years.

Following the late summer victories of 1776, royal forces held the vital city of New York until November 1783. Throughout the war various Loyalist provincial corps conducted desultory raids against the enemy in New York, New Jersey, and along the New England coast. For a time in 1777, the central department became a divided command. In the successful Philadelphia campaign, the Queen's Rangers were praised "for their spirited and gallant conduct" at the battle of Brandywine Creek on 11 September 1777.[17] In the attempt to link with Burgoyne near Saratoga, Fort Clinton and Fort Montgomery on the Hudson River were attacked and captured on 6 October 1777. The Loyal American Regiment was prominent in this action.

The following year, the Prince of Wales American Regiment and the King's American Regiment were part of the royal force that defeated a French and American rebel expedition at the battle of Rhode Island on 29 August. In the summer of 1779 a Massachusetts-inspired expedition against British and Loyalist forces at Fort George on the Penobscot River, near present-day Castine, Maine, was smashed. For their part royal forces raided Connecticut in

1779 and 1781. In the second expedition Loyalist Benedict Arnold and his American Legion, along with elements of the New Jersey Volunteers and other units, sacked New London and Groton, captured Fort Griswold, and massacred part of the rebel garrison on 6 September 1781. This was the last major action of the war in this theatre of operations.

St. Augustine, the key centre for the British and Loyalist forces in the southern department, remained virtually unthreatened throughout the war. In the colonial South generally, however, the hostilities of the civil war mounted with increasing fury from the summer of 1775 until several months after the surrender of Lord Charles Cornwallis at Yorktown. Towards the end of the first year of armed conflict, a royal force in Virginia, including the Queen's Own Loyal Virginia Regiment and the Ethiopian Regiment, complete with the inscription ''Liberty to Slaves'' emblazoned across their chests, rashly attacked the rebels near Norfolk, and were soundly defeated at the battle of Great Bridge on 9 December 1775. Nonetheless, the battle embodied a philosophical contradiction in the struggle for American liberty, for only when loyal Blacks reached the British lines did they begin to feel, as Boston King wrote: ''the happiness of liberty, of which I knew nothing before''.[18] Black Loyalists fought throughout the war as soldiers and seamen, cooks and couriers. Their military contribution was important, yet their hopes for a ''promised land'' under British authority proved illusory.

Two months after the battle of Great Bridge, a large contingent of North Carolina Loyalists,

mostly Scotch Highlanders en route to join the British at Wilmington, was caught and destroyed at Moore's Creek Bridge on 27 February 1776. As armed Loyalist opposition in South Carolina and Georgia had collapsed earlier, the loyal Americans throughout the colonial South were forced to confine their military activities to minor skirmishes and harassing raids for nearly the next three years.

In 1778 British strategy for suppressing the rebellion was significantly altered. Nova Scotia and Québec appeared secure and the New York theatre of operations was at least in a stalemate. The British were convinced that the southern colonies were essentially loyal. They firmly believed that substantial numbers of loyal Americans in Georgia and the Carolinas would eagerly rally to the royal standard if the British army provided vigorous support. A major royal offensive from New York was launched in December against Savannah; the town fell quickly and easily. A second British and Loyalist expedition from St. Augustine, spearheaded by East Florida Rangers seeking revenge, completed the re-establishment of royal authority in Georgia. In the Carolinas, loyal Americans mustered in considerable numbers to join the royal victors in Georgia, but at Kettle Creek, they were attacked and defeated by backcountry rebels on 14 February 1779. Royal forces counterattacked and smashed rebel resistance in Georgia at Briar Creek on 3 March 1779.

In October 1779 a French and American rebel amphibious force attempted to storm Savannah. The royal forces, including the Georgia Loyalists, the King's (Carolina) Rangers, the 1st Battalion of DeLancey's Brigade and the 3rd Battalion of New Jersey Volunteers were well entrenched around the town, and inflicted severe casualties on the enemy attackers who soon retreated. The following spring, emboldened by the successes in Georgia, a second major royal force from New York sailed south, and forced the surrender of Charleston on 12 May 1780. The Queen's Rangers, British Legion, King's American Regiment, New York Volunteers, and elements of DeLancey's and other Loyalist provincial corps took part in this victory. Over five thousand men, half of them continentals, were taken prisoner in the worst disaster for the colonial rebels during the whole war. In a pursuit and follow-up action, the British Legion destroyed a retreating rebel force at Waxhaw on 29 May 1780.

The civil war and strife now became very bitter in the Carolinas. A premature gathering of loyal Americans to join the British invasion of North Carolina was frustrated in vicious fighting at Ramsour's Mill on 20 June 1780. At Hanging Rock on 6 August 1780, the Prince of Wales American Regiment was nearly annihilated in a four-hour battle. These actions spurred the British to advance into the interior to support the "good Americans". They seemed to succeed. The British Legion, Volunteers of Ireland, and Royal North Carolina Regiment played a prominent rôle in the crushing royal victory at the battle of Camden on 16 August 1780. Two days later the British Legion thrashed rebel partisans at Fishing Creek. However, at isolated backcountry places like Musgrove's Mill, Wahab's Plantation, Black Mingo Creek, Blackstock's, Rudgeley's Mill, and Hammond's Store, loyal Americans suffered defeats as the "evil rage[d] with more violence than ever".[19]

The watershed for the military fortunes of the British and Loyalists in the colonial South was the battle of King's Mountain on 7 October 1780. Here on the western borders of the Carolinas, the King's American Regiment, Loyal American Regiment, American Volunteers, and some New Jersey Volunteers took a terrible beating from backcountry rebels. With the exception of Major Patrick Ferguson, the battle was fought solely by colonial Americans.

At Cowpens, the British Legion and the royal forces were overwhelmingly defeated in a second disaster on 17 January 1781. The British were becoming discouraged. Without adequate provisions, the army had campaigned "in the most barren inhospitable, unhealthy part" of the southern backcountry, and had opposed "the most savage, inveterate, perfidious, cruel enemy, with zeal and with bayonets only".[20] Following another unsuccessful major engagement at Guilford Court House on 15 March 1781, Cornwallis surprisingly turned away from the Carolinas, and marched his exhausted and frustrated troops towards Virginia and Yorktown. Thus, the southern strategy was terminated and the loyal Americans of the South were abandoned.

In spite of the departure of Cornwallis, the colonial Americans continued and intensified the civil war. Although the rebels began to capture interior posts and force the British and Loyalists to retreat to their coastal bases, the British post at Ninety-Six in South Carolina, garrisoned by elements of DeLancey's Brigade and the New Jersey Volunteers, stoically withstood a siege through May and June 1781. After the hard-fought battles of Hobkirk's Hill on 25 April 1781 and Eutaw Springs on 8 September 1781, however, the British and Loyalists in the south were virtually confined to Savannah, Charleston, and other ports.

This did not mean that the fighting in the interior ceased. At Hillsboro, North Carolina, for example, loyal Americans under the inspired leadership of the redoubtable Colonel David Fanning captured the rebel governor and took more than two hundred prisoners in a classic surprise attack early on the morning of 12 September 1781. Later in the day Fanning checked the pursuing rebels in a sharp action at Lindley's Mill on Cane Creek.[21] During the following months, the surrender of Cornwallis at Yorktown and the news of a preliminary peace were ignored, and the civil war in the South continued unabated until both sides realized that if there was to be no stop "to these massacres the country will be depopulated".[22] By the spring of 1783, the southern Loyalists, now concentrated at St. Augustine, engineered a last act of defiance: under the command of Andrew Deveaux of South Carolina, they attacked and captured Spanish-held Nassau in the Bahamas.

In the colonial South, as in other theatres, the British had underestimated the strength and, perhaps, the devotion of the loyal Americans. In the South particularly, the British were unable to supply the loyal Americans with the necessary arms and supplies for conducting extended campaigns against rebel forces. But time and again, groups of overzealous loyal Americans mustered prematurely to support the royal cause. Invariably, they were surprised and defeated in some backcountry location practically inaccessible to the British army. For their part, the loyal Americans lacked a united and coordinated leadership, and were frustrated as much by their isolation in scattered parts of the interior as by unreliable British military support and by the determination of the rebels. Nonetheless, especially towards the end of the conflict, the loyal Americans battled with reckless courage in a frenzied effort, not to preserve a political-constitutional ideology but to defend their families, farms, and settlements. With their existence at stake, the loyal Americans fought with muskets, bayonets, and clubs, and, when necessary, with sticks, stones, and bare hands.

These Loyalists-in-arms became a "band of brothers", who fought with skill and enterprise, and showed themselves to be "disciplined enthusiasts in the cause of their country".[23]

With the creation of the United States, the officers and men of the Loyalist provincial corps faced new challenges. Many went on to combat the wilderness of Nova Scotia, New Brunswick, and Upper Canada. Others, especially in Upper Canada, would fight the traditional republican foe again during the War of 1812. In both these struggles, the defiant success of the loyal Americans proved to be their vindication and redemption.

R.S.A.

1. Proverbs 24:21, "My Son, fear thou the Lord and the king . . . ."

2. See. W.O. Raymond, "Loyalists in Arms," *New Brunswick Historical Society Collections*, no. 5 (1904), pp. 189–223; P. Katcher, *The American Provincial Corps, 1775–1784* (Reading, Pa., 1973).

3. R.W. Coakley and S. Carr, *The War of the American Revolution* (Washington, 1975), p. 43. For a general discussion of this theme, see R.A. Bowler, *Logistics and the Failure of the British Army in America, 1775–1783* (Princeton, N.J., 1975).

4. P.H. Smith, *Loyalists and Redcoats: A Study in British Revolutionary Policy* (New York, 1972), p. 84*ff*.

5. Quoted in Katcher, *The American Provincial Corps*, p. 32; Coakley and Carr, *The War of the American Revolution*, p. 43.

6. See W.H. Siebert, "Loyalist Troops of New England," *New England Quarterly*, vol. 4 (1931), pp. 108–10.

7. J.C. Crane, "Col. Thomas Gilbert, The Leader of the New England Tories," *New England Historic Genealogical Society Publications* (1893), pp. 8–19.

8. Smith, *Loyalists and Redcoats*, pp. 14–15; E.I. Manders and R. Chartrand, "His Majesty's New-foundland Regiment of Foot (Pringle's), 1780–1783," in J.R. Elting, ed., *Military Uniforms in America: the Era of the American Revolution, 1775–1795* (San Rafael, 1974), p. 54.

9. For details see J.P. MacLean, *An Historical Account of the Settlements of Scotch Highlanders in America prior to the Peace of 1783 together with Notices of Highland Regiments and Biographical Sketches* (1900; reprinted Baltimore, 1978), especially pp. 308–24; G.F.G. Stanley, *Canada Invaded, 1775–1776* (Toronto, 1973); S.S. Cohen, ed., *Canada Preserved: The Journal of Captain Thomas Ainslie* (Toronto, 1968); "Letter-book of Captain Alexander McDonald, of the Royal Highland Emigrants, 1775–1779," *New York Historical Society Collections*, vol. 15 (1882), pp.205–498.

10. For details see E.A. Cruikshank, "The King's Royal Regiment of New York," *Ontario Historical Society Papers and Records*, vol. 27 (1931), pp. 193–323; M.B. Fryer, *King's Men: the Soldier-Founders of Ontario* (Toronto, 1980) pp. 63–128.

11. E.A. Cruikshank, *The Story of Butler's Rangers and the Settlement of Niagara* (1893; reprinted Owen Sound, 1975); Fryer, *King's Men*, pp. 124–78.

12. B.G. Loescher, *Rogers Rangers: The First Green Berets* (San Mateo, Ca., 1969), pp. 179–201; The Jessup Papers, Ontario Archives; E.R. Stuart, "Jessup's Rangers as a Factor in Loyalist Settlement," *Three History Theses* (Toronto, 1961); The John Peters Narrative, Metropolitan Toronto Library; Fryer, *King's Men*, pp. 237–62, 179–204, 204–29, and 230–36.

13. Raymond, "Loyalists in Arms," p. 204.

14. W.S. Stryker, *The New Jersey Volunteers (Loyalists) in the Revolutionary War* (Trenton, N.J., 1887).

15. J. Mollo and M. McGregor, *Uniforms of the American Revolution* (London, 1975), p. 36; Smith, *Loyalists and Redcoats*, pp. 63–66.

16. See R.S. Allen, "The Loyalists of Atlantic Canada," *Loyalist Gazette* (Spring 1982), p. 5.

17. H.M. Jackson, "The Queen's Rangers, 1st American Regiment," *Journal of the Society for Army Historical Research*, vol. 14 (1935), pp. 147–48.

18. For details see J. St. G. Walker, *The Black Loyalists: the Search for a Promised Land in Nova Scotia and Sierra Leone 1783–1870* (New York and Halifax, 1976), pp. 1–2*ff*.

19. For details see Coakley and Carr, *The War of the American Revolution*, pp. 121–25.

20. F. and M. Wichwire, *Cornwallis and the War of Independence* (London, 1970), p. vii.

21. L.S. Butler, ed., *The Narrative of Col. David Fanning* (Davidson, N.C., 1981), pp. 54–56.

22. Katcher, *The American Provincial Corps*, p. 34.

23. J.G. Simcoe, *Simcoe's Military Journal* (first published London, 1784; Toronto, 1962), p. 133.

**8. Map of the battles of
the American rebellion,
1775–1783**

**9. The Loyalist Provincial
Corps, 1775–1783**
Hand-coloured photograph of a
painting by Thomas D. Masey
18.4 cm × 33.0 cm

New Brunswick Museum, Saint
John
No. W.1028

Loyalist Provincial Corps were raised during the
rebellion to assist the British cause. This picture
is one artist's conception of the uniforms worn
by several of these units.

**10. Allan Maclean of
Torloisk**
Artist unknown
British
Ca. 1775
Miniature on ivory
4.1 cm × 3.5 cm

The Lord Maclean, London

Allan Maclean of Torloisk (1725–1798), Isle of
Mull, Scotland, fought with the Jacobites in
1745–1746. After the defeat at Culloden, he was
forced to flee but returned to Great Britain in
1750 when an amnesty was granted to Jacobite
officers willing to swear allegiance to the
Hanoverians.

Maclean saw important service in North
America with the Royal American Regiment
(62nd, later 60th Foot) during the Seven Years'
War (1756–1763). He was severely wounded at
Carillon in 1758; he took part in the capture of
Fort Niagara in 1759, and during that same summer he joined General James Wolfe's army
besieging Québec. Maclean returned to Britain
in 1761.

In 1775 Maclean was authorized to raise a
loyal regiment of disbanded Highland soldiers
who had settled in North America and of recent
Scotch emigrants. These men became the Royal
Highland Emigrants, comprising two battalions,
with Maclean as lieutenant colonel commandant
of the regiment and in personal command of the
1st Battalion. This battalion played a notable
part in the crucial defence of Canada against the
invading colonial rebels during the winter of
1775–1776.

In the spring of 1776 Maclean became adju-
tant general of the British Army, and a year later
military governor of Montreal with the rank of
brigadier general. He returned to Britain following the peace of 1783 and retired from the army
in 1784. He lived in London until his death in
1798.

Like Allan Maclean, John Small (1726–1796), a native of Perthshire, Scotland, served with the Scots Brigade of the Dutch army before obtaining a commission in the 42nd Royal Highland Regiment in 1747. He came to North America with his regiment and settled there after the Seven Years' War.

In 1775 Small received a major's commission to raise and command the 2nd Battalion of the Royal Highland Emigrants in Nova Scotia and Saint John's Island (Prince Edward Island). Part of the 2nd Battalion was assigned to garrison duty in Nova Scotia. In November it relieved Fort Cumberland, besieged by a motley force of colonial rebels under Jonathan Eddy. The rest of the batallion, including Small, served in the southern theatre, in Charleston in May 1780 and in Eutaw Springs in September 1781.

John Small rose to the rank of major general and later served as lieutenant governor of the Island of Guernsey.

11. John Small
Henry R.S. Bunnett
Canadian
4th quarter, 19th century
Oil on canvas, from a miniature of unknown date
30.7 cm × 25.9 cm

McCord Museum, Montreal
No. M-730

The uniform of the Royal Highland Emigrants was similar to that of the 42nd Highland Regiment: full Highland garb and short red coat with royal blue facings. The sporran of the 84th was made of racoon skin instead of the usual badger.

12. Officer of Royal Highland Emigrants
Robert J. Marrion
British
1976
Watercolour on paper
35.8 cm × 23.2 cm

Canadian War Museum, Ottawa
No. 75028

13. Camp colour, Royal Highland Emigrants

Ca. 1776
Wool, blue
36.8 cm × 41.9 cm

Canadian War Museum, Ottawa
No. 1961-51

When the Army marches, the Quarter-Masters and the camp-colour-men are ordered before to take up the ground on which they are to encamp; . . . they are to mark out the encampment of their Regiments, and when that is done, they are to make their necessary-houses, and to get them finished, if possible, by the time the Regiments arrive, that the camp may be kept sweet and clean.

(Humphrey Bland, *A Treatise of Military Discipline . . .*, 1762)

A regulation of 1768 specified that camp colours were to be "eighteen inches square [46.0 cm × 46.0 cm] and the colour of the Facing of the Regiment, with the number of the Regiment upon them". The Royal Highland Emigrants were placed on the British regular establishment as the 84th Foot on 1 April 1779; thus this colour precedes that date. This specimen is 16" × 14½" (42.0 cm × 37.0 cm), smaller than the dimensions prescribed by the warrant of 1768.

Alexander Fraser (*ca.* 1729–1799) had been a lieutenant in the 78th Foot (Fraser's) during the Seven Years' War. He settled in Quebec when his regiment disbanded in 1763. In 1779 Fraser became a captain in the Royal Highland Emigrants, just after the regiment had been included on the army establishment as the 84th. After the regiment was disbanded in 1783, Alexander Fraser, as a veteran officer on half pay, was permitted to appear on ceremonial occasions in this uniform.

14. Uniform coat of Captain Alexander Fraser, 84th Foot
British
Ca. 1792
Wool, scarlet with blue facings, gold lace

McCord Museum, Montreal
No. M-17764

The "RP" inscribed on the buttons of John Leggett's coat stands for "Royal Provincials". This device, rather than a specific regimental one, was worn by the members of many Loyalist units throughout the rebellion. Following the hostilities, Leggett settled in Nova Scotia.

15. Uniform Coat of John Leggett, Royal North Carolina Volunteers
British
Ca. 1775–1783
Wool, scarlet with blue facings, gold lace

Public Archives of Nova Scotia, Halifax
No. AC 70.3

16. Thayendanegea, Joseph Brant, Mohawk chief

George Romney
English
1776
Oil on canvas
127.0 cm × 101.6 cm

National Gallery of Canada, Ottawa
No. 8005

Thayendanegea (1743–1807) was born in the Ohio country and moved with his widowed mother to the Mohawk Valley a few years before the Seven Years' War. As an adolescent he served with the British forces during the war. In 1761 he was brought to Sir William Johnson who, impressed with the young man's abilities and potential, arranged for him to attend Moor's Indian Charity School at Lebanon, Connecticut, where he remained for two years.

At the start of the colonial rebellion, Brant sailed to England as part of a delegation on Indian affairs. It was during this journey that he sat for the Romney portrait. Romney (1734–1802) was, with Reynolds and Gainsborough, a fashionable painter of his time. Brant attracted wide attention in London social circles, particularly when dressed in the full regalia of a tribal chieftain. Romney painted Brant in the romantic tradition of his century, as the classical noble warrior.

Following his return to America, Brant commanded a mixed Indian-White force of loyal volunteers. He campaigned actively along the New York-Pennsylvania frontier throughout the war. In 1784 Brant led Mohawk Loyalists and other Iroquois of the Six Nations Confederacy to the Grand River in Upper Canada.

These wampum credentials were worn by Thayendanegea as ambassador of the Six Nations to the British government in 1776. Each comprises a necklace of purple wampum, nine white wampum beads, and three silver brooches mounted on fringed leather strips. The Turtle Clan was Thayendanegea's; the Wolf Clan, his wife's.

17. Wampum credentials of the Turtle Clan
North American
7.4 cm × 12.4 cm

McCord Museum, Montreal
No. M-1899

18. Wampum credentials of the Wolf Clan
North American
7.6 cm × 22.2 cm

McCord Museum, Montreal
No. M-1898

John Johnson (1742–1830), son of Sir William Johnson, fought his first campaign alongside his father in the Seven Years' War. Shortly after inheriting his father's vast estates in the Mohawk Valley of upper New York province in 1774, Johnson was forced to flee because of his Loyalist sympathies. About two hundred of his loyal tenants, chiefly Scotch Highlanders, followed him in a gruelling wilderness trek to Quebec.

The party reached Montreal in June 1776, and almost immediately Governor Sir Guy Carleton authorized Johnson to raise and command the King's Royal Regiment of New York. Known as the Royal Yorkers, the unit was recruited largely from among Johnson's tenants and other loyal Americans who had been forced to flee the Hudson and Mohawk valleys. The Royal Yorkers played an important part in the northern campaigns of the rebellion.

19. Sir John Johnson, Bart
Francesco Bartolozzi
Engraving, in A.S. DePeyster, *Miscellanies*, 2nd ed., New York, 1888, plate CLXII
9.2 cm × 7.6 cm

The Library, Public Archives of Canada, Ottawa
No. F567 D41

See also no. 4.

20. Uniform of Lieutenant Jeremiah French, 2nd Battalion, King's Royal Regiment of New York
British
Jacket wool, scarlet with blue facings, gold lace; waistcoat and breeches wool; reproduction hose and shoes

Canadian War Museum, Ottawa
No. 1983–92

In 1777 Provincial corps were initially issued green coats with various facings. Waistcoats, breeches, hats, and accoutrements were the same as regular army issue. By the 1778 campaign, however, it was decided to clothe the provincials, like the regulars, in scarlet coats.

Jeremiah French served as a lieutenant in the 2nd Battalion, KRRNY, which was raised in 1780. This uniform is of particular interest as it is rare to find so complete a uniform of this period, including the original breeches. These are held up by a linen tape laced in the rear, and have a ''fall'' in the front.

21. Jeremiah French's powder horn
Upper Canada
1792
Animal horn
31.0 cm

Mr. Robert Adams, Burlington, Ontario

The horn bears the inscription "I. French June The 13 1792".

22. Ensign Samuel Mackay, 2nd Battalion, King's Royal Regiment of New York
Eugène Hamel
Québec
Ca. 1782
Gouache on paper
23.0 cm × 17.7 cm

Musée du Québec, Québec
No. A-54.282-D

**23. Lieutenant Colonel
Isaac Allen**
Artist unknown
Ca. 1780
Watercolour miniature on paper
3.8 cm × 6.4 cm oval

New Brunswick Museum, Saint
John
No. 62.7

**24. Side Drum of 2nd
Battalion, New Jersey
Volunteers**
British
Ca. 1776
Oak and parchment
H. 43.9 cm; Diam. 43.9 cm

New Brunswick Museum, Saint
John
No. 23761

Three battalions of this regiment constituted the
largest single Loyalist provincial contingent to
come to New Brunswick in 1783–1784. Many
New Jersey Volunteers settled on regimental
land grants in the Parish of Kingsclear, York
County.

With the success of the British in the Long Island campaign of 1776, British prestige among loyal Americans rose substantially. They began flocking to the royal standard. The New Jersey Volunteers was raised at New York. With six battalions, it was the largest provincial regiment of the war.

Before the rebellion, Isaac Allen (1741–1806) was a lawyer in Trenton, New Jersey. When hostilities broke out, Allen received a commission in the New Jersey Volunteers. He rose to command its 2nd Battalion. At the close of the war, Allen moved his family first to Wilmot, Nova Scotia, then to a regimental land grant he was awarded at Kingsclear, New Brunswick. As a lawyer in the newly formed province, Isaac Allen achieved prominence as a judge of the Supreme Court and as a member of the New Brunswick Executive Council.

25. Folding field chair used by Lieutenant Colonel Isaac Allen
Ca. 1780
Oak
H. 72.3 cm; W. 67.2 cm; Diam. 36.2 cm

New Brunswick Museum, Saint John
No. 10570

26. James Moody
Photograph of a lost painting

Courtesy Mr. John Wentworth Moody, Ottawa

27. James Moody's Commission as Ensign, 1st Battalion, New Jersey Volunteers, 1778
32.5 cm × 24.4 cm

Mr. John Wentworth Moody, Ottawa

Like many Americans, James Moody (*ca.* 1744–1809) was "a Lover of Peace, good Order, and loyal on Principle". Initially he had no thoughts of taking part in the revolutionary conflict, but from 1777 he began to suffer harassment with respect to his allegiance, and was forced to flee, with more than seventy loyal neighbours, to the British lines.

As an officer in the New Jersey Volunteers, Moody was frequently employed to lead small parties of men deep into rebel territory to observe rebel movements, enlist other loyal Americans, and generally annoy the inhabitants. He was subsequently recognized as a "Case of great Merit and great Exertions in his Majesty's Service", and received handsome compensation from the Loyalist Claims Commission.

28. Lieutenant James Moody's Narrative of his Exertions and Sufferings in the Cause of Government, since the Year 1776; Authenticated by Proper Certificates
London, 2nd edition, 1783
12.7 cm × 20.8 cm

Mr. John Wentworth Moody, Ottawa

Though the account of Moody's adventures was not generally believed, it doubtless helped its author when he went before the Loyalist Claims Commission in 1784. He received nearly £3000 in compensation and half pay as a lieutenant when the New Jersey Volunteers were disbanded after the war.

29. "Lieutenant Moody Releases a Condemned Prisoner from Sussex c[o]. Gaol, May 1780"
Photographic reproduction, original engraving by Robert Pollard
19.6 cm × 14.7 cm

Mr. John Wentworth Moody, Ottawa

This incident was only one of a number of dramatic exertions described by James Moody in his *Narrative . . .* (see no. 28). The Sussex County Gaol was located in Newton, northwestern New Jersey.

30. Lieutenant Colonel John Graves Simcoe
Photographic reproduction of a painting by Jean-Laurent Mosnier

By permission of the Metropolitan Toronto Library Board, Toronto

Although the general cut and the lace of this long-tailed coat date from 1775–1783, the coat itself is from the post-rebellion period. As a veteran officer on half pay, William Jarvis wore it at dinners, balls, and on other occasions.

When it was decided to change the uniform of the Loyalist corps from green to scarlet, the Queen's Rangers, along with several other corps, sought to preserve the green. The Rangers' commander, John Graves Simcoe, wrote that green was the colour best suited to North American conditions: ''If put on in the spring, by autumn it nearly fades with the leaves, preserving its characteristic of being scarcely discernible at a distance''.

31. Coat of William Jarvis, Queen's Rangers
Ca. 1783
Wool, green with velvet facings

Toronto Historical Board, Old Fort York, Toronto
No. 64-230-23

32. A hussar and light infantryman of the Queen's Rangers
Photographic reproduction of a watercolour drawing by Captain Murray in Lieutenant Colonel John Graves Simcoe's *Journal of the Operations of the Queen's Rangers . . .* (1787)

Canadian War Museum, Ottawa

**33. Mrs. Arianna
Chalmers Saunders**
Attributed to John Rising
English
Ca. 1789
Oil on canvas
71.5 cm × 92.0 cm

New Brunswick Museum, Saint
John
No. W.6996

John Saunders (1754–1834) was born in Virginia of a family whose forebears fought on the Royalist side in the English Civil War. During the rebellion, he raised a troop of horse, and joined the Queen's Rangers as a cavalry captain. He is portrayed here wearing the uniform of that corps.

In 1783, when his two large estates in Virginia were confiscated, Saunders went to England, where he studied and then practised law. In 1790 he was appointed to the Supreme Court of New Brunswick. He became chief justice in 1822.

34. Captain John Saunders
Attributed to John Rising
English
Ca. 1789
Oil on canvas
71.5 cm × 91.5 cm

New Brunswick Museum, Saint John
No. W.6995

John Morrow, a farm hand from Oyster Bay, New York, joined the Queen's Rangers as a private soldier. He began a diary on 1 September 1779 and continued it even after his discharge on 13 September 1780. He recorded his final entry on 24 August 1781.

35. John Morrow's Diary
Manuscript, 84 pages,
1779–1781
19.2 cm × 15.5 cm

Macdonald Stewart Foundation, Montreal
No. 973.3/M83/1779-81

36. Sword of Major Robert Rogers

Mid-eighteenth century
Silver hilt
L. 74.3 cm

Royal Ontario Museum, Toronto
No. 975.84

Robert Rogers (1731–1795) grew up on the frontier of New Hampshire. There he had much contact with the Indians and was exposed to Indian raids. During the Seven Years' War, he led a ranger unit and fought extensively in the Lake Champlain theatre.

Rogers led a dissolute life and was considered to be a man of few principles. It was said that he might have fought on either side of the rebellion. As it turned out, he offered his services first to the rebels, who imprisoned him. He escaped and presented himself at the British headquarters in New York in August 1776. He was made a lieutenant colonel and ordered to raise and command a battalion known as the Queen's American Rangers. When the poor state of this unit was discovered, Rogers was retired on half pay. Later in the war, the unit achieved distinction under the leadership of John Graves Simcoe as the Queen's Rangers.

In 1779 Rogers founded the King's Rangers, but he soon lost the command to his brother James, as alcoholism made it impossible for him to function as commander. Robert Rogers returned to England, where he died in 1795.

37. Officer's small sword

British
1759
Steel blade with silver hilt
L. 106.5 cm

Mr. Warren Moore, Greensboro,
North Carolina

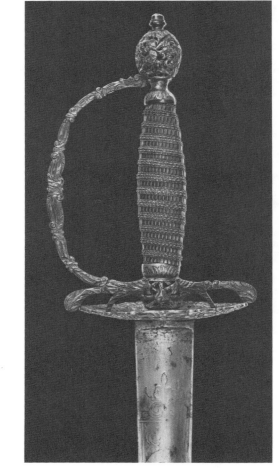

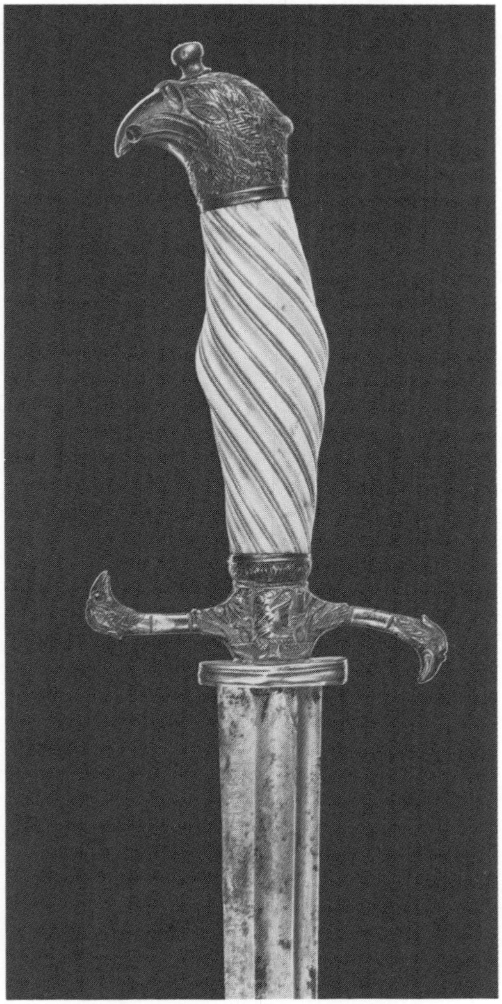

38. Officer's hanger with eagle-head pommel
Probably American
Ca. 1780
Steel blade with silver hilt and fluted ivory grip
L. 86.8 cm

Mr. Warren Moore, Greensboro, North Carolina

39. Officer's small sword
J. Crum
British
1755
Steel blade with sharkskin grip
L. 97.9 cm

Mr. Warren Moore, Greensboro, North Carolina

40. Hunting sword with dog-head pommel
Ephraim Brasher
American
Ca. 1770
Steel blade with silver hilt and
green-tinted fluted grip
L. 77.0 cm

Mr. Warren Moore, Greensboro,
North Carolina

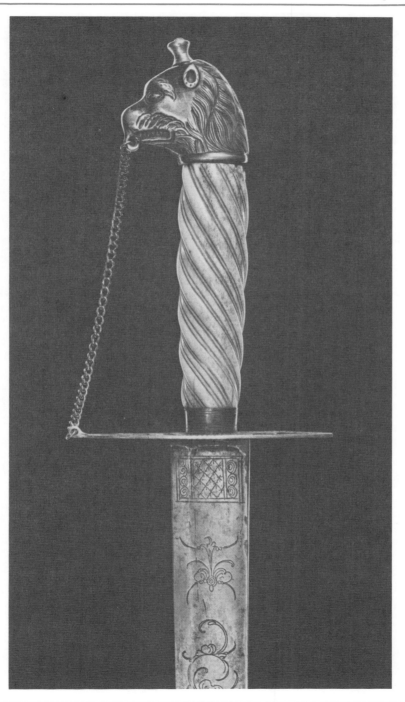

**41. Officer's sword with
lion-head pommel**
Steel blade with silver hilt and
fluted ivory grip
L. 94.2 cm

Mr. Warren Moore, Greensboro,
North Carolina

David Fanning (1755-1825)

David Fanning was born in Virginia and grew up in North Carolina. By 1773 he was settled in western South Carolina. Fanning was a zealous partisan of the royal cause and fought desperately and spectacularly throughout the bitter conflict in the Carolinas. In July 1781 he was appointed a colonel of the Loyal Militia of North Carolina.

After the rebellion, Fanning departed for the new Loyalist province of New Brunswick, where he was elected to the Legislative Assembly. In 1800 he moved to Digby, Nova Scotia.

42. Fanning family Bible
British, The Society for
Promoting Christian
Knowledge
No date
21.7 cm × 13.8 cm

Mr. Harold Denton, Digby,
Nova Scotia

The Bible is opened at an inscription written by David Fanning:

. . . born in Amelia County in the province of Virginia on the 25th day of October 1755 and Sarah Fanning my wife was born in Randolfsh County, formerly call.[d] Orrang County in the province of North Carolina on the 17th day of March 1766 . . . .

43. David Fanning's cartridge box, shoulder-strap type
British
Ca. 1775
Leather over hardwood block
24.5 cm × 16.0 cm

Mr. Lister Fanning Trask,
Digby, Nova Scotia

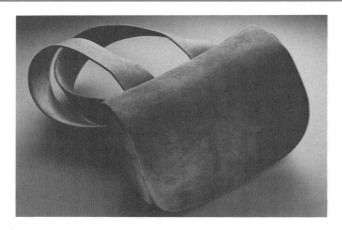

44. David Fanning's naval telescope
T. Harris & Son
London
1st half 19th century
Objective tube L. pushed in
35.0 cm; L. drawn out 85.0 cm;
Diam. 6.0 cm

Mr. Harold Trask, Nepean,
Ontario

Benjamin Thompson (1753–1814), a native of Massachusetts, was an articulate and impressive young man with an inventive turn of mind, a penchant for things military, and a strong sense of loyalty to the royal cause.

Following the British evacuation of Boston in 1776, Thompson made his way to England, where he immediately became a favourite of the Secretary of State for the Colonies, Lord George Germaine. Shortly thereafter Germaine appointed him undersecretary of state in the American department.

Late in 1781, with the downfall of his mentor imminent, Thompson returned to America to assume command of the King's American Dragoons. Landing in Charleston after the defeat at Yorktown, he was unable to reach his troops in New York, and had to be content with some minor skirmishes in the final stages of the rebellion.

At the war's end, Thompson returned to Europe and travelled on the continent. At the request of Karl Theodor, Elector of Bavaria, he entered the Palatine-Bavarian civil service in 1784. As minister of war for a decade, he was responsible for numerous reforms in the Bavarian army. In 1792 the Elector elevated him to count—Count Rumford, after the early name for Concord, New Hampshire. Thompson retired in 1798, going first to England, then to France, where he devoted the last years of his life to scientific experiments. He died in 1814 in Auteuil, a Paris suburb.

45. Benjamin Thompson, Count Rumford

Artist unknown
Oil on canvas
51.4 cm × 62.1 cm

Bayerisches Armeemuseum, Ingolstadt, Federal German Republic
No. A 2394

46. Second guidon of the King's American Dragoons
British
Silk, metallic fringe, silk and metallic embroidery
76.0 cm × 69.0 cm

New Brunswick Museum, Saint John
No. 58.92

The Second . . . Guidon, of each Corps, to be of the Colour of the Facing of the Regiment, with the Badge of the Regiment in the Centre . . . within a Wreath of Roses and Thistles on the same stalk. . . . The White Horse, on a Red Ground, to be in the First and Fourth Compartment, and the Rose and Thistle conjoined upon a Red Ground, in the Second and Third Compartments. . . .

Those Corps which have any particular badge are to carry it in the Centre.

(Royal Warrant, 19 December 1768)

The uniform facing of the King's American Dragoons was blue, much faded on this relic. The "LD" in the centre of the regimental badge signifies "Light Dragoons".

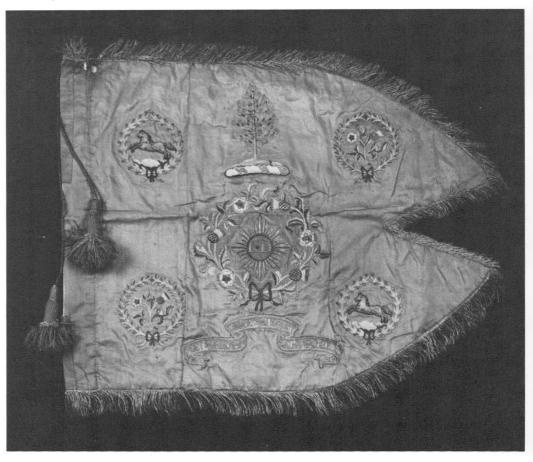

The inscription on the blade reads:

As a lasting testimony of friendship, esteem & affection, this sword is presented to Ben. Thompson Esqr. by the Corps of Officers appointed to the Royall Regiment of Highland Emigrants raisd in North America in 1775.

47. Sword presented to Benjamin Thompson by officers of the Royal Highland Emigrants
Ca. 1777
L. 101.0 cm

Musée de l'île Sainte-Hélène, Montréal
No. 76.2.13

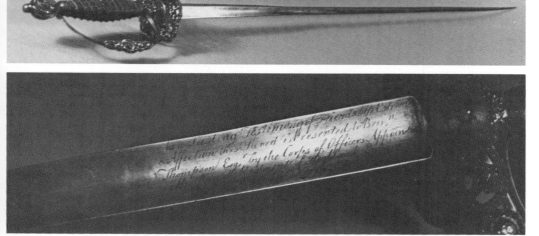

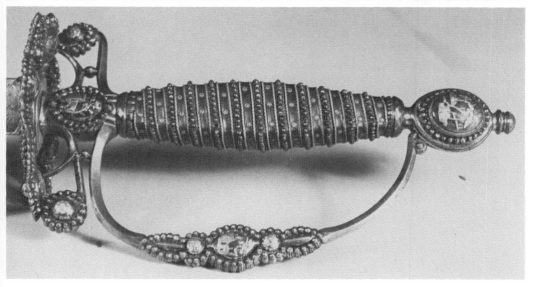

48. Experimental mortar developed by Count Rumford
Bavarian
1780s–1790s
Bronze mortar and wood carriage
Mortar 37.1 cm × 29.5 cm;
Diam. at muzzle 17.9 cm;
carriage 102.0 cm × 41.5 cm

Bayerisches Armeemuseum, Ingolstadt, Federal German Republic
No. A 2395

49. Rumford lamp
Probably British
Early nineteenth century
36.0 cm (glass chimney missing)

New Brunswick Museum, Saint John
No. 30372

Benjamin Thompson, Count Rumford, was a gifted scientist who in 1779, at the age of twenty-six, earned a fellowship in the Royal Society. His particular area of scientific interest was experimenting with light and heat. This experimental mortar dates from his Palatine-Bavarian career; the Rumford lamp probably was developed after his retirement.

50. Monument to Count Rumford in the English Garden in Munich
Simon Warnberger
German School
1796
Etching
23.0 cm × 29.0 cm

Staatliche Graphische Sammlung, Munich, Federal Republic of Germany
No. 97744

One of Benjamin Thompson's most important military reforms in Bavaria was the establishment in 1789 of a vegetable garden in Munich for the benefit of the soldiers. The monument to Rumford was erected by friends in Munich around 1795. An inscription reads:

> Halt your step, Stroller! Gratitude will enhance your enjoyment. A creative suggestion from Karl Theodor (Elector of Bavaria) interpreted by the vigorous intellect of Rumford, the humanitarian, with feeling and love, has transformed this once barren area into what you now see before you.

Benedict Arnold (1741–1801) was born in Norwich, Connecticut, and served as a boy in the Seven Years' War. In 1775 he joined the rebellion, and proceeded to record his many exploits, which marked him as perhaps the most natural military leader of the revolutionary war. After helping to capture Ticonderoga in 1775, he led a column 560 km over the gruelling Kennebec-Chaudière route to Quebec. There he joined Richard Montgomery's column in a surprise attack on 31 December 1775; however, American losses were heavy.

After the American withdrawal from the province of Québec, Arnold lost the flotilla he had built on Lake Champlain. He played an important rôle in the rebel victory at Saratoga in 1777. In 1778, following the departure of the British, he was named governor of Philadelphia; later he was given command of the American post at West Point.

It was here in September 1780 that Benedict Arnold crossed over to the British lines and joined the army as a brigadier general. He immediately raised the American Legion, which he led on numerous raids in Virginia and then in Connecticut.

51. Benedict Arnold
Artist unknown
English
1776
Hand-coloured mezzotint
engraving, published by
Thomas Hart
35.4 cm × 25.0 cm

New Brunswick Museum, Saint
John
No. W.86

52. Colonel James DeLancey

Artist unknown
Oil on wood
24.0 cm × 17.8 cm oval

Mr. George DeLancey Hanger,
Roanoke, Virginia

James DeLancey (1747–1804) was the nephew of General Oliver DeLancey, who raised and commanded DeLancey's Brigade. At the start of the rebellion James was High Sheriff of Westchester County, New York, and colonel of the county militia. From the latter in 1777 he raised a troop of light horse called the Westchester Chasseurs, which harassed and raided rebel positions around New York. In 1780 DeLancey commanded the Westchester Refugees ("DeLancey's Cowboys"), a mixed Loyalist unit of light horse and infantry.

After the rebellion, James DeLancey settled in Annapolis County, Nova Scotia, where he became a prominent landholder and farmer. He was active in the militia, and was elected to the provincial Legislative Assembly for Annapolis County. Later he was appointed to the Legislative Council. He died at his farm in Round Hill, Annapolis County in May 1804.

Banastre Tarleton (1754–1833) came to America in 1776 as a cornet in the 16th Light Dragoons. Three years later he was commander of a Loyalist provincial corps of mounted troops, the British Legion (Tarleton's Legion). Cruel, vain, brave, and coldly effective, Tarleton boasted of having butchered more men than anyone else in the army. Though he made heavy demands on his men, he was greatly admired by them.

Tarleton's tactics were almost always based on speed, surprise, impact, and vicious sabring. At Waxhaw, South Carolina, on 29 May 1780, his men nearly annihilated a superior force of col-onial rebels. At this engagement killing men who offered to surrender became known as "Tarleton's quarter".

Tarleton's prestige and terror in America waned somewhat after his defeat at the Cowpens in January 1781. In Britain, however, he remained a celebrity. He sat for what is unquestionably one of Sir Joshua Reynolds' most celebrated portraits, and he was subsequently returned to Parliament on several occasions.

53. Lieutenant Colonel Banastre Tarleton
J.R. Smith, after a painting by Sir Joshua Reynolds
British
1782
Mezzotint engraving
64.1 cm × 40.0 cm

Anne S.K. Brown Military Collection, Providence, Rhode Island
No. GB-MP1782 lf-1

A dragoon carbine was equipped with a ring-and-bar fitting which allowed the trooper to attend to his mount with both hands without losing his weapon.

54. Dragoon carbine
British
1760–1770
133.4 cm overall

Mr. Warren Moore, Greensboro, North Carolina

The sling swivels denote that this flintlock piece had a military use. The decorative brass furniture and fine quality suggest that it was carried by an officer.

55. Blunderbuss
William Walsingham
British
Ca. 1770
81.3 cm overall

Mr. Warren Moore, Greensboro, North Carolina

56. Light dragoon horse pistol

British
1761
41.3 cm overall

Mr. Warren Moore, Greensboro,
North Carolina

57. Dragoon's cartridge belt

American
1770s
Leather with tin cartridge inserts
and steel buckles
L. 95.5 cm; greatest W. 9.5 cm

Mr. Warren Moore, Greensboro,
North Carolina

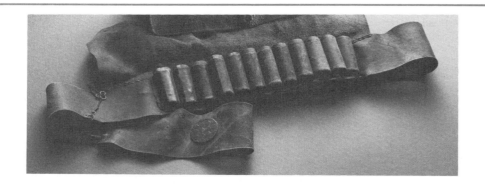

58. Sabre and scabbard, frog, waist-belt, and shoulder strap

American
Ca. 1755
Steel blade with brass hilt and
maple grip; scabbard, frog,
waist-belt, and shoulder strap
leather with brass fittings
L. of sabre 97.9 cm; L. of
scabbard 82.5 cm

Mr. Warren Moore, Greensboro,
North Carolina

59. Dragoon's sabre

Blade German
Ca. 1740
Steel blade and steel basket-type
hilt, wood grip
L. 115.5 cm

Canadian War Museum, Ottawa
No. 1977-484/4

The initials "JMK" at the top of the plate were presumably engraved by the user.

60. Shoulder-belt plate of the King's Royal Regiment of New York
Ca. 1776
Silver
7.7 cm × 6.3 cm oval

Mr. J.E. Kelly and Nor'westers and Loyalist Museum, Williamstown, Ontario No. 969.10.1

On the reverse is the hand inscription, "1780, Fannings Regt. Dragoons". Edmund Fanning (1737–1818) raised the King's American Regiment in 1776, and served as its colonel. He was subsequently lieutenant governor of Nova Scotia from 1783 to 1786, and of Saint John's Island (Prince Edward Island) from 1787 to 1804.

61. Shoulder-belt plate of the King's American Regiment
Ca. 1780
Gilded brass
7.3 cm × 4.8 cm

Mr. John Wentworth Moody, Ottawa

62. Shoulder-belt plate of Butler's Rangers
British
Ca. 1777
Brass
6.5 cm × 5.0 cm oval

Canadian War Museum, Ottawa
No. 1983-114/1

63. Shoulder-belt plate of the 4th Battalion, New Jersey Volunteers
Ca. 1776
Silver
7.5 cm × 5.0 cm

New Brunswick Museum, Saint John
No. 23162

This plate was worn by Lieutenant Justus Earle (1749–1825). He was twice captured and exchanged during the rebellion. Earle settled in Queens County, New Brunswick, after the war. This piece is curious in that it bears the initials ''JE'' in place and in the style of the Royal Cypher.

64. The Siege of Rhode Island, taken from M^r. Brindley's House on the 25th August, 1778
British
Coloured lithograph from *The Gentleman's Magazine*, February 1779
25.5 cm × 20.1 cm

Canadian War Museum, Ottawa
No. 1982-581/3

The Prince of Wales American Regiment and the King's American Regiment were part of the royal force that defeated a superior French and rebel expedition at the battle of Rhode Island.

65. Uniform button thought to be of King's Rangers
Ca. 1780
Silvered brass
Diam. 2.4 cm

Canadian War Museum, Ottawa
No. 1980-978

The Queen's Rangers were included on a new American establishment as the 1st American Regiment in 1779.

66. Officer's uniform button of 1st American Regiment (Queen's Rangers)
Nutting King
Covent Garden, London
1779
Pewter
Diam. 2.2 cm

Canadian War Museum, Ottawa
No. 1980-978/954

67. Other ranks' uniform button of Royal Provincials
Ca. 1776
Pewter
Diam. 2.2 cm

Canadian War Museum, Ottawa
No. 1980-978/1404

68. Other ranks' button of 84th Regiment of Foot (Royal Highland Emigrants)
1779
Pewter
Diam. 2.3 cm

Canadian War Museum, Ottawa
No. 1980-978/1238

69. Other ranks' uniform button of Butler's Rangers
Ca. 1780
Pewter
Diam. 1.6 cm

Canadian War Museum, Ottawa
No. 1980-978/1409

70. Uniform button of Roman Catholic Volunteers
1777–1778
Pewter
Diam. 1.4 cm

Canadian War Museum, Ottawa
No. 1980-978/1412

The Roman Catholic Volunteers were raised in Philadelphia in October 1777. A year later (October 1778) four companies were merged into the Volunteers of Ireland.

71. Officer's uniform button of King's Royal Regiment of New York
1770s
Gilded brass
Diam. 2.3 cm

Mrs. H.H. Winter, Ottawa

Long arms in the Rebellion

The basic weapon of the foot soldier on both sides of the colonial rebellion was the smooth-bore flintlock musket. By the 1770s there were many musket varieties and several innovations.

An infantryman in the line of battle was expected to load and fire four rounds a minute.

At best, his accuracy was limited to about fifty metres. Typically, each side exchanged two or three volleys before the side with the advantage launched a bayonet charge, which was substantially more devastating than musket-fire.

The Long Land musket, with its forty-six-inch barrel, was first manufactured in 1717 and remained in regular issue as an infantry firearm of the British army until 1768. It was called the Long Land to distinguish it from the Short Land service musket (forty-two-inch barrel) issued to the dragoons *ca.* 1720.

Although the Long Land musket had been replaced by a lighter model by the beginning of the rebellion, many Loyalist provincial corps still carried the older weapon. This example belonged to a soldier in the 3rd Battalion, New Jersey Volunteers. The tang of the butt-plate is engraved "Reid", and the top of the barrel, "3 Bt N.J.V".

72. Long Land service musket
British
1760s
155.8 cm overall

Dr. D.R. MacInnis,
Shubenacadie, Nova Scotia

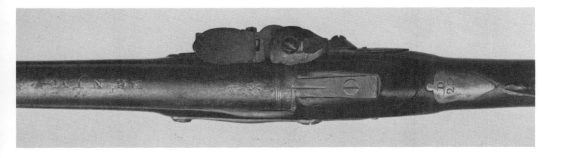

The new-pattern musket, with its shorter, forty-two-inch barrel was adopted by Royal Warrant in 1768. A shorter, lighter and less costly firearm than the Long Land musket had long been desired; and it had become customary to cut four inches from the Long Land service muskets that had worn thin at the muzzle. By the time of the rebellion, all regular units of the British Army and an increasing number of the Loyalist provincial corps had been equipped with the Short Land new pattern musket.

73. Short Land new-pattern musket
British
Ca. 1775
147.5 cm overall

Canadian War Museum, Ottawa
No. 1983-114/2

74. Flintlock fowling piece
Manufactured by George Jones
English
Ca. 1740
135.7 cm overall

Canadian War Museum, Ottawa
No. 1981-296/7

The lock was later converted from flint to percussion.

75. Flintlock fowling piece
Attributed to Jeremiah Smith
New England
Pre-1775
185.4 cm overall

Mr. Warren Moore, Greensboro,
North Carolina

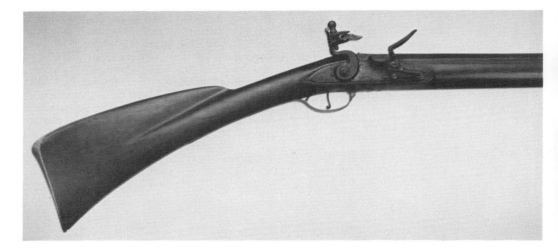

These fowling pieces are typical of the many types of personal weapons that were used by both sides in the early weeks of the rebellion. Since they had been used previously for hunting, relatively few were equipped with bayonets. The bayonet would become important as both sides eventually adopted the formal European tactics used by armies ranged on open ground.

76. Committee of Safety Musket
American
1775 or 1776
148.2 cm overall

Mr. Warren Moore, Greensboro,
North Carolina

At the start of hostilities, gunsmiths throughout the Thirteen Colonies were contracted by local committees of safety to produce muskets for the rebels. Though each colony issued its own specifications, the muskets produced resembled the British patterns, with barrel lengths varying from forty-two to forty-six inches, and bores of about 0.75 mm.

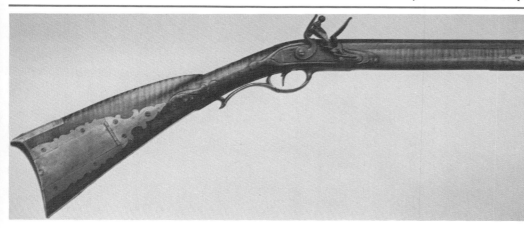

77. Kentucky rifle
Manufactured by Wolfgang
Haga
American
1780s
160.6 cm overall

Mr. Warren Moore, Greensboro,
North Carolina

Around 1740 American gunsmiths of German
origin had developed an arm with a rifled barrel. Known as the American, the Kentucky, or
the Pennsylvania rifle, it was inspired by the
German *jaeger* (huntsman) rifle. Rifling usually
consisted of seven spiral grooves, which gave the
lead ball a twist, or rotation, and greatly increased the projectile's accuracy. A good
rifleman could hit an enemy soldier at 300
metres. The American rifle was well adapted to
the irregular tactics of wilderness warfare. This
specimen, though not used in the rebellion, is
an exquisite example of the type of gun used
by many of the rebels.

78. Canteen
American
1770s
Wood
W. 10.0 cm; Diam. 13.6 cm

Mr. Warren Moore, Greensboro,
North Carolina

79. Musket
Manufactured at Potsdam
Arsenal
Prussian
Ca. 1775–1781
155.7 cm overall

Canadian War Museum, Ottawa
No. 1976-240

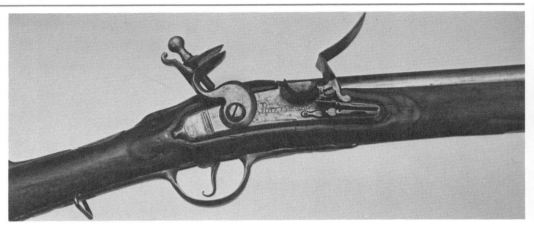

Firearms of this type were used in the rebellion
by German troops in the British service.

80. Musket
Manufacture royale de
Maubeuge
French
1763 model
154.0 cm overall

Canadian War Museum, Ottawa
No. 8-4-20b

After the British-pattern muskets used by both
sides, the most common muskets were those
manufactured in France. The rebels imported
large numbers of French muskets, including this
one, which is stamped ''US'' on the lock plate.

81. Ferguson Rifle
Manufactured by D. Egg
British
Ca. 1776
120.7 cm overall

Mr. Warren Moore, Greensboro,
North Carolina

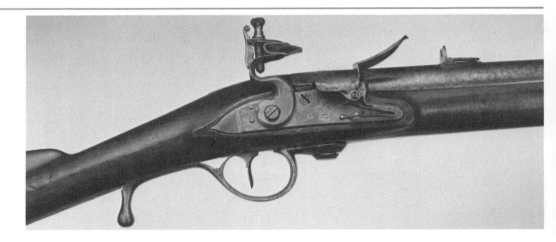

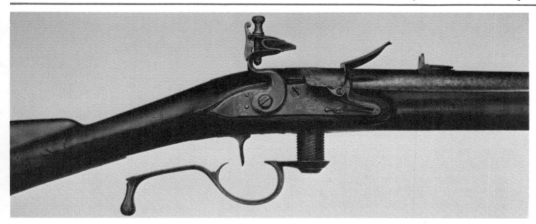

The most tangible advantage of Patrick Ferguson's breech-loading rifle was that it could be loaded while the soldier was lying on the ground. By only one rotation of the threaded plug on the trigger guard, the breech was opened and the ball dropped into the cavity. With the rifle pointing slightly downward, the ball rolled to a stop; the rest of the breech cavity was then filled with powder and the plug closed. The rifle was also less vulnerable in bad weather than were conventional weapons.

The Ferguson was an efficient rifle, quick to load and fire, and superior to the traditional musket. Major Ferguson demonstrated his new rifle at the Royal Military Academy, Woolwich, in June 1776, and he patented his invention the following December. Despite its advantages, however, the Ferguson rifle was not generally adopted. Only about two hundred of them were manufactured, most for use in the American rebellion.

Though the traditional Amerindian war club (no. 83) continued to be used, iron-headed tomahawks and belt axes of European manufacture, which arrived with the Europeans in the sixteenth century, were more efficient weapons and well suited to war under North American conditions. They were used as late as the War of 1812, not only by Indians (no. 82) but also by Canadian irregulars during the French regime, Loyalist Provincial Corps, and light infantry units of the regular British Army (no. 84).

82. Tomahawk
French
Ca. 1760
Iron head, wooden haft
43.5 cm × 16.0 cm

Canadian War Museum, Ottawa
No. 1975-113

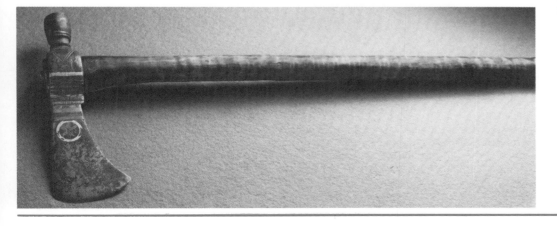

83. War club

Mohawk
Ca. 1775
Wood
51.0 cm × 12.5 cm

Royal Ontario Museum, Toronto
No. HD 6629

84. Belt-axe head

Ca. 1775
Iron
13.5 cm × 7.0 cm

Mr. Victor Zabatiuk, Cornwall,
Ontario

The cheek of this axe is marked $\frac{13[}{62}$, referring to the 3rd Company 62nd Regiment of Foot, which suffered heavy losses at the Battle of Saratoga in October 1777. ''IW'' beneath the crown on the blade refers, perhaps, to the maker.

85. Side drum of Royal Provincials

British
Ca. 1776
Oak and parchment
H. 44.0 cm; Diam. 44.0 cm

King's Landing Historical
Settlement, Fredericton
No. M 75.210

''Royal Provincials'' was a general designation applied to loyal American units raised in the early months of the colonial rebellion. Although a more formal regimental system was developed, much of the equipment of the Royal Provincials continued to be used. The device—a crown over the initials R.P.—is in gold on a black oval ground.

Cartridge Boxes and Powder Horns

The regular soldier of the period used cylindrical cartridges wrapped in paper. These he carried in a cartridge box, a block of hardwood with vertical holes, covered with leather. The box was held either over the right hip by a shoulder strap (no. 87) or in front on a waist belt (nos. 86 and 89).

After the advent of cartridge boxes, the powder horn remained popular among civilians who joined the Loyalist Provincial Corps. The horn was easily obtainable from slaughtered cattle; it was light, strong, and watertight. It was a popular pastime for owners to scrimshaw, that is, inscribe designs, illustrations, and names on their horns.

86. Cartridge box, waist-belt type
British
1770s
Leather over hardwood block
22.4 cm × 9.8 cm

Canadian War Museum, Ottawa
No. 4-3-40

87. Cartridge-box plate of Butler's Rangers
British
Ca. 1777
Brass
7.4 cm × 5.1 cm

Canadian War Museum, Ottawa
No. 1978-529/5

88. Cartridge box, shoulder-strap type
American
1770s
Leather over hardwood block
23.7 cm × 9.0 cm

Mr. Warren Moore, Greensboro, North Carolina

**89. Colonel Edward
Jessup's cartridge box and
waist belt**
British
1770s
Leather over hardwood block,
waist belt leather
21.6 cm × 11.5 cm

Fort George National Historic
Park, Niagara-on-the-Lake,
Ontario
Nos. FA.69.44A, FA.69.44B

Colonel Edward Jessup organized the King's
Loyal Americans. In 1781 this unit became part
of the Loyal Rangers (Jessup's Corps).

**90. William Hazen's
powder horn**
North American
1761, with subsequent
alterations
Animal horn
36.0 cm

New Brunswick Museum, Saint
John
No. 59.72

This horn bears scrimshaw of ''the invasion
route New York to Montreal''. The attractive
silver fittings were added, perhaps early in the
nineteenth century.

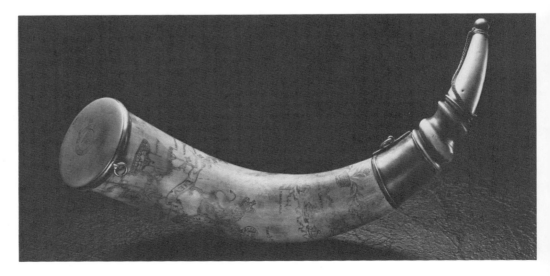

This horn bears scrimshaw of armorial bearings, and the frontier regions of the Hudson-Mohawk drainage region.

91. Powder horn
North American
Ca. 1775
Animal horn
35.5 cm

McCord Museum, Montreal
No. M-6931

The scrimshaw on this horn represents "The countries conquered by the Five Nations, 1756–63".

92. Powder horn
North American
Ca. 1763
Animal horn
36.0 cm

McCord Museum, Montreal
No. M-6936

93. Powder horn
United States
4th quarter 18th century
32.4 cm

Canadian War Museum, Ottawa
No. 1970-192

This ornate horn, deeply carved with scenes of the rebel assault on Québec on 31 December 1775, is said to have been executed by a "monk of la Trappe," who was allegedly a former rebel soldier.

Gorgets

The gorget, the last vestige of mediaeval armour, was worn by eighteenth-century officers as a symbol of rank. It hung about the neck on a ribbon the colour of the regimental facing or was attached by rosettes to the collar buttons. The Royal Clothing Warrant of 1768 specified that gorgets were to bear the Royal Arms, a custom widespread before that date (no. 94).

The 1768 warrant also specified that the designation of line regiments of the British Army was to be engraved on the gorget along with the Royal Arms. This appears only rarely on those of the loyalist Provincial Corps, which generally were not numbered regiments. An exception was the King's American Regiment, which in 1781 was included on a new American establishment as the 4th American Regiment (no. 96). The crest incorporating the Royal Cypher was of regimental design and unofficial.

---

94. Gorget, with Royal Arms
British
Ca. 1760
Gilded brass
13.9 cm × 11.4 cm

McCord Museum, Montreal
No. M-212

---

95. Gorget, with Royal Arms
British
4th quarter 18th century
Gilded brass
10.8 cm × 8.8 cm

Mr. John Wentworth Moody, Ottawa

This gorget belonged to Ensign (later Lieutenant) James Moody of the New Jersey Volunteers.

96. Gorget of the King's American Regiment
British
1781
Gilded brass
12.1 cm × 11.5 cm

Metropolitan Museum of Art, New York
No. X.5

The design of this gun corresponds to that of a fowling piece. Yet the presence of a socket bayonet suggests that it was intended for use as an officer's fusil. The bayonet is stored in the stock; access is provided by pressing the button at the bottom of the butt tang.

97. Officer's fusil
Manufactured by Daniel Moore
British
1770
132.2 cm overall

Mr. Warren Moore, Greensboro, North Carolina

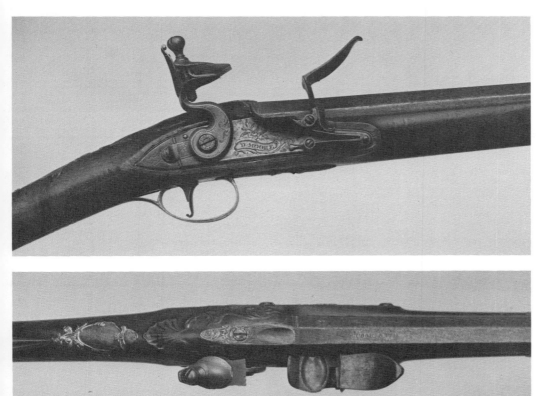

98. Pair of officer's holster pistols
Manufactured by Daniel Moore
British
1774
30.5 cm overall

Mr. Warren Moore, Greensboro,
North Carolina

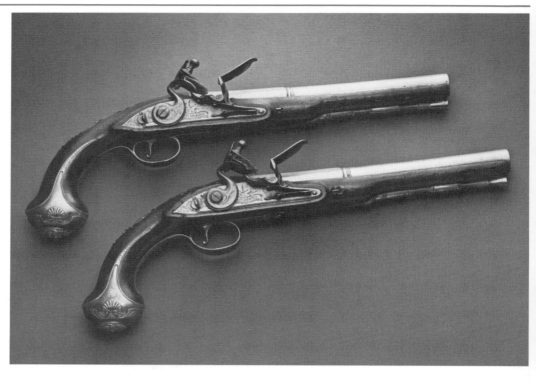

99. Pair of saddle holsters for flintlock pistols
British
Ca. 1750
Leather
L. 35.9 cm

Mr. Warren Moore, Greensboro,
North Carolina

The Evacuations
by Robert S. Allen

The civil war and rebellion in colonial America was over. The British and the Loyalists had suffered defeats at Saratoga, King's Mountain, and Yorktown, and had won victories at Long Island, Charleston, and Camden. Yet the final result was the loss of imperial unity, the creation of a new nation, and the uprooting of thousands of loyal Americans who became political refugees. For the officers, men, and families of the Loyalist provincial corps, the irreconcilable hatred engendered during the war years removed any thought of returning to their former homes and neighbours.

By the spring of 1783, along the Atlantic seaboard, only St. Augustine and New York remained under royal authority. Yet St. Augustine ceased to be a haven for the loyal refugees when East Florida was returned to Spain under the Treaty of Paris. Eventually, many southern Loyalists established plantations in the British West Indies, especially at Nassau in New Providence and throughout the Bahama Out-Islands. Others opted for the potential of British North America, and these St. Augustine Loyalists took passage throughout the summer of 1784 for Nova Scotia, where they settled at Chedabucto Bay and along the rough and mostly barren lands of the eastern shore of the province.[1]

New York was the key evacuation port for the loyal Americans. Between April and November 1783, five major fleets transported as many as thirty thousand refugees to various locations in Nova Scotia, and to what later became the "Loyalist Province" of New Brunswick.[2] The sea voyages were dangerous. One ship, the *Martha*, with the Maryland Loyalists and part of the 2nd Battalion of DeLancey's Brigade on board, was wrecked on a ledge of rocks at the approaches of the Bay of Fundy, and more than one hundred people perished.[3]

Many of the loyal Americans who did arrive safely were not overjoyed at the prospects. At Port Roseway, the site of the future town of Shelburne on the south shore of Nova Scotia, a fleet of "upwards of thirty sail" carrying about three thousand loyal refugees "hove in sight" on Sunday, 4 May 1783. What many passengers saw as they looked at their new home were "dark woods and dismal rocks".[4] From the deck of the *Two Sisters*, Sarah Frost peered out at the terrain surrounding the St. John River on 18 May 1783, "Loyalist Landing Day" in New Brunswick. "It is, I think, the roughest land I ever saw," she wrote.[5] Yet Edward Winslow, the muster-master General of the Loyalist provincial corps, thought the same view was "positively the most magnificent and romantic scene I have ever beheld", and considered the St. John River and valley as "the pleasantest part of this country".[6]

The loyal refugees were naturally fearful, anxious, suspicious, and physically and emotionally drained. The recollections of one Loyalist woman typified the sentiments of most of the recently arrived refugees. After landing at the mouth of the St. John River, she climbed to the top of Chipman's Hill "and watched the sails disappear in the distance, and such a feeling of loneliness came over me that 'though I had not shed a tear through all the war I sat down on the damp moss with my baby on my lap and cried bitterly.'"[7]

But the loyal Americans had arrived, and the impact of their arrival and settlement on the future dominion of Canada was to be profound, unique, and permanent.

R.S.A.

1. "List of People at Chedabucto," 6 April 1785, and "Farm Lots laid out for Loyal Emigrants and Disbanded Corps, between 21 May 1783 and 31 December 1786," PANS, RG 1, vol. 223, nos. 107 and 146; "A List of the British Legion and other Loyalists at Guysborough," 8 September 1784, PANS, RG 1, vol. 359, no. 66; T.H. Raddall, "Tarleton's Legion," *Nova Scotia Historical Society Collections*, vol. 28 (1947), pp. 1–50; J.L. Wright, Jr., *British St. Augustine* (St. Augustine, 1975); A.C. Jost, *Guysborough Sketches and Essays* (Guysborough, 1950), pp. 117–77.

2. For Nova Scotia prior to the partition of 1784 see "Return of Loyalists gone from New York to Nova Scotia," 12 October 1783, PANS, RG 1, vol. 369, no. 198; Governor J. Parr to Governor F. Haldimand, Halifax, 14 June 1784, *ibid.*, vol. 367, no. 31; Parr to Shelburne, 24 January 1784, A.G. Doughty, ed., *Report of the Public Archives for the year 1921* (Ottawa, 1922), p. 364. For peninsular Nova Scotia after the partition of 1784 see M. Ells, "Settling the Loyalists in Nova Scotia," *Canadian Historical Association, Report for 1934*, pp. 105–9; M. Gilroy, comp., *Loyalists and Land Settlement in Nova Scotia* (Halifax, 1937). For New Brunswick see E.C. Wright, *The Loyalists of New Brunswick* (Fredericton, 1955); R. Fellows, "The Loyalists and Land Settlement in New Brunswick, 1783–90," *Canadian Archivist*, vol. 2 (1971), pp. 5–15.

3. Wright, *Loyalists of N.B.*, pp. 85–87.

4. See G. Clopper to C. Whitworth, New York, 18 April 1783, PANS, MG 1, The White Collection, vol. 948, no. 193; W.O. Raymond, "The Founding of Shelburne: Benjamin Marston at Halifax, Shelburne and Miramichi," *New Brunswick Historical Society Collections*, no. 8 (1909), p. 210; J. Courtney to A. Cunningham, Port Roseway, 1 July 1783, PANS, MG 1, White Collection, vol. 948, no. 210.

5. "The Diary of Sarah Frost," in W.O. Raymond, ed., *Kingston and the Loyalists of the "Spring Fleet" of A.D. 1783 . . . .* (Saint John, 1889), p. 30.

6. E. Winslow to W. Chipman, River St. John's, 7 July 1783, W.O. Raymond, ed., *The Winslow Papers* (Saint John, 1901), pp. 266–67. The Winslow Family Papers, the most extensive collection of Loyalists papers in Canada, are housed in the Provincial Archives of New Brunswick (Fredericton). For the Loyalist journey and arrival, see also "Loyalist Transport Ships, 1783," *New Brunswick Historical Society Collections*, no. 5 (1904), pp. 273–79.

7. W.H. Nelson, *The American Tory* (Oxford, England, 1961), p. 169.

**100. Minute of Cabinet
advising the evacuation
of the American Colonies,
30 March 1782**
Reproduction, original in Royal
Archives, Windsor
By permission of Her Majesty
the Queen

By the spring of 1782, the British government had accepted the principle of the independence of the Thirteen Colonies. Cabinet advised George III that the garrisons at New York, Charleston, and Savannah should be evacuated, and that Sir Guy Carleton, commander-in-chief of British forces in America, should make this his first priority. The minute is in the hand of William Petty Fitzmaurice, Earl of Shelburne, Secretary of State for the Colonies.

New York was the key evacuation port for the Loyal Americans, and throughout the summer and autumn of 1783 the city was caught up in the frenzied activity of the departing British Army and Loyalists.

101. Box
Mid-eighteenth century
Walnut with brass handle
L. 23.1 cm; H. 13.3 cm;
W. 13.3 cm

Mr. and Mrs. George Bruce,
Shelburne, Nova Scotia

102. Sir Guy Carleton
Artist unknown
Probably British
Ca. 1780
Oil on canvas
76.2 cm × 63.5 cm

The Earl and Countess of
Malmesbury, Basingstoke,
Hants, England

Guy Carleton (1724–1808) entered the British army as ensign in the 25th Foot in 1742. He achieved distinction in the course of five appointments in North America between 1759 and 1796.

At the start of the colonial rebellion, as lieutenant governor of Québec, Carleton defended the province against the rebels. Though as a military commander his handling of the invasion (apart from the defence of the city of Québec) was hesitant and indecisive, the enemy was routed from the province by the spring of 1776. Carleton returned to England in 1778.

In 1782 Carleton took over Sir Henry Clinton's command. Benevolent, humane, and competent, he made careful arrangements for the evacuation of thousands of Loyalist provincial troops and civilian refugees. He adamantly resisted American demands for a precipitate removal from New York, which would have meant abandoning hundreds of Loyalist families to their fate in the infant republic.

Of all government officials, Sir Guy Carleton, the "kindly autocrat", did most to ease the plight of the Loyalists.

This copy of the famous Mitchell map is known as the "White map", after James White, a noted Canadian geographer from the 1880s to the 1920s. Included on the map are inscriptions and boundary tracings prepared by White as evidence in the deliberations over the 1926 boundary dispute between Canada and Newfoundland.

John Mitchell was a physician and botanist living in Virginia when he began his map of North America around 1750. This map, the only one Mitchell produced, proved to be a masterpiece of eighteenth-century cartography. During the twenty years that followed its appearance in 1755, the map was frequently consulted as a reference in deliberations to establish boundaries in British North America. It served as the principal cartographic instrument in the 1783 Versailles negotiations of the boundary with the United States.

103. "A Map of the British and French Dominion in North America . . ."
First published in 1775
John Mitchell
135.2 cm × 194.9 cm

National Map Collection, Public Archives of Canada, Ottawa
No. 10,000-1755(1774)(1782)

104. "Smith's Celestial Globe"
English
Late 18th century
Diam. 61.0 cm and 65.0 cm

New Brunswick Museum, Saint John
No. X 7512

105. Slant-front desk
Québec
Ca. 1786–1796
Mahogany and pine
H. 108.8 cm; W. 105.5 cm;
Depth 52.5 cm

History Division, National
Museum of Man, Ottawa
No. D-2582

This desk was made in Lower Canada for Sir
Guy Carleton during his term as governor-in-
chief of British North America (1786–1796).

**106. Tory Refugees on
their Way to Canada**
Howard Pyle
Reproduced from *Harper's
Magazine*, Dec. 1901

Courtesy Delaware Art Museum,
Wilmington, Delaware

Loyalist Military Settlement in Nova Scotia and Prince Edward Island

by Phyllis R. Blakeley

Provincial Archivist for Nova Scotia
Public Archives of Nova Scotia, Halifax

South aspect of Halifax Nova Scotia &c &c in 1780 - by E Hicks

During the year 1783 the population of Nova Scotia doubled as twenty thousand disbanded Loyalist troops and refugees arrived. Providing shelter, food, and a livelihood for these immigrants was a formidable task. Fortunately, the British army had the capacity to provide rations and tools, and the commissary's department expanded its depots. Unfortunately, the parts of the province best suited to earning a living had already been settled, and tracts of land left for the Loyalists—along the south-east coast in Shelburne, Halifax, and Guysborough counties, along the Northumberland Strait and in part of Digby and Annapolis counties—too often had beautiful views but rocky soil.

The efficient Commander-in-Chief in Nova Scotia, General John Campbell, took the initiative needed. He ordered that the distribution of rations be continued, and a muster of disbanded soldiers and refugees be undertaken to determine those entitled to the "Royal Bounty of Provisions and Necessities".

In September 1783, at Port Roseway, later named Shelburne, disbanded men from various British regiments and provincial corps joined the refugees and the civilian Loyalists, who had organized themselves into the Port Roseway Associates. The new town had been established that summer. Its population of five thousand was soon to double and it became the fourth city in North America after Philadelphia, New York, and Boston. "In six months time there were upwards of 800 houses built, and most of them of the very wood that grew where the town now stands. Here are at present from 1400 to 1500 houses, and some of them as good as any in the Province."[1] Some of the troops disbanded at Shelburne arrived early in September, but most did not come until the twenty-third. They were settled chiefly in Parr's division at the north end, and drew their lots on 22 November. Soldiers of 41 military corps settled at Shelburne: 1311, including their families, were from 24 British regiments; Loyalist provincial corps totalling 210, including their families, were from 16 Loyalist provincial corps. Some of the 3rd New Jersey Volunteers went to Shelburne with their commander, Lieutenant Colonel Abraham Van Buskirk, who was grateful to be able to live in Benjamin Marston's cellar the first winter.

Both regular British regiments and the provincial corps were to be disbanded at Halifax, the only naval and army base left on the coast of British North America. In October, nine British regiments of the line and detachments from eight others sailed for England, leaving behind those who wished to accept the King's offer of free land.

Nova Scotia was garrisoned by British regiments and provincial corps: the Royal Fencible Americans (Goreham's Corps) had defended Fort Cumberland in the Eddy Rebellion; the King's Orange Rangers were at Fort Hughes, Cornwallis; the 84th Regiment was stationed at Fort Edward in Windsor; the King's Rangers and the St. John's Volunteers served on St. John's Island (Prince Edward Island); the Royal Garrison Battalion and the Royal Nova Scotia Volunteer Regiment were garrisoned at Halifax, Sydney, and Charlottetown.

The Nova Scotia Volunteers and the Royal Garrison Battalion received orders to disband on 10 October 1783. Although they were discharged ten days later, they were allowed to remain in their barracks until a transport could take them to their allotted land. The Royal Garrison Battalion went to Sheet Harbour, where 122 were living in the summer of 1784.

Captain Timothy Hierlihy, Jr., son of the lieutenant colonel of the Nova Scotia Volunteers, chose fertile wooded land on the north shore, near Antigonish, on the Northumberland Strait with intervals along the river. The Volunteers sailed that autumn with a year's rations for 111; they built huts, cut wood, and hunted. Farm lots and lots in the town, named Dorchester, were drawn on 8 June 1784.

When Lieutenant Charles Stewart mustered the Nova Scotia Volunteers in July 1784 to determine the number and location of those eligible for the "Royal Bounty of Provisions", he found only sixty in residence. He disqualified fifty-one men who had gone to St. John's Island and fifteen men who were away fishing and not entitled to rations since they were not clearing farms. Dorchester failed to develop because men could not build a town and at the same time clear their farms. Gradually the community moved upriver to the present site of Antigonish.

A company of the 84th or Royal Highland Emigrants had been garrisoned at the blockhouse at Fort Edward. Captain Allan MacDonald of Kingsburgh, who had raised soldiers for the 84th in North Carolina, arrived in 1778. (His wife Flora, the rescuer of Bonnie Prince Charlie, joined him for "one of the worst winters ever seen there" but because of ill health left for Skye in October 1779.)

Others serving in the 84th Battalion had been recruited as they arrived from Scotland. Their vessels were boarded before reaching port and the able-bodied Scottish emigrants—sometimes father and sons together—were "persuaded" to enlist at Boston. Their wives and children were taken to Halifax and cared for by the army.

The 2nd Battalion of the 84th disbanded at Windsor. Commanding officer Major John Small received a blanket grant of 105 000 acres east of Windsor along the Minas Basin in Douglas Township, Hants County. Covering the districts of Nine Mile River, Gore, and Kennetcook, the grant was in trust for John Small and his regiment. Small paid £24.6.11 "for conveying the Women, children and provision of the 2nd Battalion from the public stores at Windsor to the lands located to the Regiment".[2] In the 1784 muster, Lieutenant Charles Stewart found 307 disbanded soldiers at Newport and "Kennetcoot", of whom 289 were entitled to provisions.

Many men of the 84th became discouraged because Major Small returned to England, where he died before his soldiers received their final grants. Having sold their provisions, the soldiers worked as day labourers on Windsor-area farms, which were part of the estates owned by officials and merchants of Halifax. The soldiers' titles were finally settled in 1816 with a new grant from the Crown. Those who remained to obtain titles still have many descendants in the county: Dalrymple, Ettinger, Fraser, Grant, Hennigar, Laffin, McCulloch, MacDonald, MacDougall, McPhee, Scott, Thompson, and White.

The provincial corps were also settled on the eastern shore of Nova Scotia. On 3 November 1783, 144 South Carolina Royalists, 140 King's (Carolina) Rangers, and 216 members of the Royal North Carolina Regiment disembarked at Halifax and were quartered at Point Pleasant. They had come from St. Augustine, East Florida, under the general command of Major James Wright, son of the former Governor of Georgia. On the same day, Captain John Legett, a former merchant and officer of the Royal North Carolina Regiment, obtained permission from William Nesbitt to build a house or shed on a lot in the north end of Halifax and to carry it away "whenever you are inclined to remove".[3]

On 14 November 1783, Commander-in-Chief Sir Guy Carleton ordered further provisions for the British-American corps who had chosen to settle in Nova Scotia, and the Carolinians may have received some of these supplies. The soldiers settled at Country Harbour or Stormont in December 1783, when the *Nymph* landed about three hundred southerners. The snow was dug away, trees felled, and huts built. They had brought with them some provisions, tools, and garden seeds, but one vessel was lost at sea with a large part of their supplies. Nova Scotia Governor Parr reported a mild winter, "which is very fortunate . . . particularly for the Disbanded Soldiers, who went so late upon their lands".[4]

But in the driving rain of the January thaws, water soaked through the brush roofs of their cabins. Some replaced the roofs with overlapping, split tree trunks. Many caught cold, some died of pneumonia, and all ate boiled dulse to prevent scurvy. There were fights and drunken brawls, a town lot was bartered for a pint of rum, and some settlers left as soon as they could in the spring.

When William Shaw arrived for the muster in June 1784, he found at Country Harbour about 201 men, 26 women, 21 children, and 41 servants. The settlers were building whaleboats for the fisheries because Country Harbour was the best harbour on the eastern shore between Halifax and Canso. American vessels had taken 30 000 quintals of fish (valued at 12 shillings a quintal) off the coast and had hired local inhabitants to cure them. By 1785 the people of Stormont owned 2 schooners, 6 vessels, and 12 boats for inshore fishing; they had taken 800 quintals of codfish and 3000 salmon, and had 50 000 feet of sawn lumber, 50 000 shingles, and 30 000 clapboards to sell.

Captain Legett had settled with ten in his family and three black servants. He built a fine two-storey house called "The Willows", but the hurricane of 1811 knocked down the timber in the forest and the waves swept away his house, barns, and warehouses.

About 150 men of another Carolina regiment, Banastre Tarleton's British Legion, were among those who had disbanded at Shelburne on 23 September 1783. Governor Parr wrote that Major George Hanger (later a friend of the Prince Regent) seemed very happy to have "Port Moutoon" allotted for his men, since they would not waste time coming first to Halifax. On 7 October, Surveyor General William Morris and a party of surveyors set out from Shelburne for Port Mouton, a shallow, sandy, and stormy bay. Although their sloop was lost with all their instruments and drawings aboard, the surveyors survived and eventually produced a beautiful plan for four miles of frontage on the bay and extending ten miles into the wilderness. The soil in the interior, which had never been surveyed, was thin and littered with granite.

At Port Mouton the British Legion was discharged on 10 October. Sergeants received fourteen shillings, privates seven. According to local tradition, the men drew their lots by picking numbered paper tickets out of a hat. The numbers had been written on the back of old commissary forms and were saved as proof of title. The settlers had a few tools and began to build log huts or sod houses with chimneys of beach stones.

During the remainder of October and November, 2081 New York-based personnel of the British Army and Navy arrived at Port Mouton. The senior officer was an energetic, efficient, and influential man, Colonel Robert Molleson, who had been wagonmaster general of the forces at New York. His right-hand man was Colonel Nathan Hubbill of the commissary-general's department. They named the settlement Guysborough. Molleson was able to obtain some food, and his men and their families survived on rations of one pound of salt pork and one pound of hard biscuits per day, supplemented with salt cod, snared rabbits, and clams dug from the creek at low tide. The sawn lumber that Molleson had obtained from the mills at nearby Liverpool was in short supply, and so were clothing and blankets. Women and children were forced to stay inside the tents and huts in winter.

Soon quarrels broke out between British Legion men and civilians from New York. By spring the Associated Departments of the Army and Navy had decided to move as soon as possible to Digby, St. Croix River or Chedabucto. On 19 May a forest fire destroyed Guysborough, and the settlers had to flee into the water to escape. When fishing vessels from Liverpool arrived with food, they were hired by Colonel Molleson to take a first contingent further eastward to Chedabucto Bay in June. Some of the men of the British Legion sailed with Molleson, some went to Digby, others settled on better land in the vicinity of their burned town or in fishing coves nearby.

The British Legion was not the only corps to encounter problems. The Duke of Cumberland's Regiment (Montagu's Corps) was commanded by Lord Charles Montagu, a son of the Duke of Manchester and former colonial governor. After the siege of Charleston, two battalions had been sent to Jamaica. From there Montagu hired two ships to bring them to Halifax, where Brigadier General Fox gave them permission to "occupy a part of the Barracks at Birch Cove", about five miles from the city.[5] There Montagu died on 3 February from tuberculosis.

The regiment encountered difficulties over supplies because the regulations only covered provisions for corps in British America, and Montagu's Corps had been in Jamaica. In the spring of 1784 at least twenty-five men went to Shelburne, where Captain Gideon White established his family. In May, 149 men (including 12 bandsmen, drummers, and fifers) sailed to Chedabucto Bay under the command of Captain Brownrigg and named the townsite Manchester. Their farm and timber lots were located deep in the roadless forest between the Strait of Canso and Chedabucto Bay five to fifteen miles from Manchester. Few settled in the town.

Friction developed among the different groups, and practically all of Montagu's men moved in search of wives, better land, and other occupations.[6] The remaining civilians changed the name of the town from Manchester to Guysborough (to replace the Guysborough destroyed by fire). In March 1788 Governor Parr wrote: "Many of the Privates sold their Lotts for a dollar or a pair of Shoes—or a few pounds of Tobacco—but most for a gallon of New England Rum and quit the Country without taking any residence."[7]

Like Shelburne, Conway (Digby) was an attractive site because it offered large tracts of unsettled land located on a harbour. It was named by the civilian settlers, Amos Botsford and the New York Associates, in honour of Admiral Robert Digby, who gave so much assistance to the loyal refugees who came to Nova Scotia. On 29 May 1784 John Robinson mustered 1295 men at Digby and remarked that "the Loyalists settled at Digby are extremely industrious".[8] Digby did not grow as quickly as expected because the local board of agents was empowered to subdivide the block grant. The resulting long delays caused many to move before titles were settled in 1801. However, the settlers enjoyed a prosperous livelihood from the fishing, shipbuilding, lumbering, and trading with the West Indies. Captain James Moody, "one of the most picturesque and gallant figures on the Loyalist side", settled at Sissiboo (Weymouth) and served in the provincial legislature for Annapolis County from 1793 to 1806.[9]

Disbanded Black Guides and Pioneers mustered at Digby in the summer of 1784 under the command of Sergeant Thomas Peters, a former slave in North Carolina. Thirty-five others mustered at Annapolis Royal under the command of Sergeant Murphy Steele. The Black Guides and Pioneers had been promised provisions and land on the same terms as the other disbanded soldiers, but they received rations only until December 1784. Thereafter, the agent refused to issue provisions unless they built roads, a job other Loyalists were not required to do.

In 1785 they were granted town lots of one acre each at Brindley Town, just outside Digby. Twice farm lots were surveyed for them, and each time the lots proved to belong to other settlers. Finally, in September 1789 Lieutenant John Greben surveyed 7500 acres for Joseph Leonard and 148 others. But without sufficient provisions from the British government, land clearing and settlement were impossible. Most of the Black Pioneers had emigrated again by the time the Digby Loyalists received titles to their land in 1801.

Similar difficulties had been experienced by the Black Pioneers who arrived in Port Roseway in the spring of 1783 to clear land and to help build military barracks. They were organized into companies under Colonel Stephen Blucke, "a mulatto of good reputation".[10] Most of the Black Pioneers settled across the harbour at Birchtown, where they were joined by refugees from Shelburne in July 1784. In Shelburne disbanded white soldiers had rioted, pulled down twenty of the Black Pioneers' houses, and driven "the Free negroes . . . out of Town because they labour cheaper than they the soldiers".[11] Throughout Nova Scotia, Black Loyalists found no "promised land" and many, in despair at not receiving what they were entitled to, emigrated with Thomas Peters to Sierra Leone.

Annapolis Royal was an important debarkation point for Loyalists and disbanded troops in 1782 and 1783 because the town had a fort, barracks, an Anglican church, and houses and barns where shelter could be found. A process of infill was taking place in the valley on both sides of the Annapolis River, and some military officers with means purchased farms at Annapolis and Granville. The farms were under cultivation but would not produce sufficient food to support them for seven or eight years. Many refugees in the Township of Wilmot were settled "seven miles from any Roads except what they have made themselves",[12] and many sold their lands and became labourers. General Timothy Ruggles received 10 000 acres at Wilmot, where he hired soldiers as labourers, and established a magnificent orchard. Colonel Thomas Barclay of the Loyal American Regiment, who was later British consul at New York, lived for a time at Wilmot. James DeLancey, colonel of "DeLancey's Cowboys", and lawyer Stephen DeLancey, lieutenant colonel of the New Jersey Volunteers, settled at Annapolis. Both became members of the provincial legislature. The King's Orange Rangers had a few grants at Parrsborough, across the basin from where they had been in garrison in Cornwallis. Others were at Aylesford.

Very few Loyalists came to Cape Breton Island because Great Britain had discouraged settlement. None of the regiments were disbanded on the island, but 46 disbanded soldiers were among the 146 Loyalists who settled there. One of these was Captain Jonathan Jones of the King's Orange Rangers of New York, who was the founder of Baddeck.

The land on St. John's Island, as Prince Edward Island was called until 1798, belonged to absentee landlords, who promised one quarter of it to Loyalists and disbanded soldiers. Some of the few that accepted the offer were from the St. John's Volunteers, the King's Orange Rangers, and the Royal Nova Scotia Volunteers, who had served in the garrison at Charlottetown. In June 1784 eighty-nine St. John's Volunteers and three King's Rangers were receiving provisions. Governor Walter Patterson sent a proclamation to Shelburne urging Loyalists to come to the island; fifty arrived on 13 September 1784 and sixty-nine on 17 September.

When Lieutenant Charles Stewart arrived at Charlottetown on 3 June 1784, he was unable to muster the disbanded soldiers because the men of the different corps were "scattered by one, two or three over the whole Island".[13] Many soldiers had sold their provisions to buy drink, and Governor Patterson himself had

bought provisions from two soldiers. The 1st Battalion of King's Rangers had drawn provisions until 24 April, and on 12 June it mustered seventy-three men, fifteen women, and twenty-six children. By the end of 1784, about five hundred Loyalists were on the island, chiefly in the Malpeque-Bedeque isthmus and on Lots 40 and 50 along the shores of Orwell Bay. But very few of the Loyalists were able to obtain title to their grants, and trouble over ownership continued for almost a century.

Two years after the Loyalist provincial corps had been disbanded in Nova Scotia, Governor Parr informed the secretary of state that the following had been settled on lands in 1784 and 1785: three battalions of Carolina Provincials, the Duke of Cumberland's Regiment, the British Legion, one battalion of Royal Nova Scotia Volunteers, the King's Orange Rangers, and Royal Fencible Americans (Goreham's Corps).

In addition, there were ninety officers who had not joined their provincial corps as settlers in New Brunswick. The 2nd Battalion of the 84th Regiment was not included because "it is not in the power of Man to satisfy their unreasonable demands" for land in Nova Scotia.[14]

In Nova Scotia there was a high percentage of regular soldiers (twenty per cent) and also of southerners (thirty per cent). Where geographic origin is known, thirty-five per cent of the Loyalist refugees were from New York, thirty per cent from the South, twenty per cent from New England, and fifteen per cent from the Middle Colonies. Out of a total of 19 362 land grants in Nova Scotia, 2029 were given to white soldiers,[15] who would number 4058 with their families. Records list 2428 departed Loyalists, but many others did not stay on their land long enough to receive a grant.

Although the Loyalist refugees and disbanded soldiers had been welcomed because of the need for both a larger population and "working people", the expansion was too rapid for the limited economic resources of Nova Scotia. Those who turned to the fisheries or who could combine farming, fishing, and lumbering were best able to secure a livelihood. When pensions became portable in 1787, officers' half-pay became important to the cash-poor economy.

There was considerable mobility both within and outside the province. For example, Captain George Bond of the Loyal Militia of South Carolina sold the 500 acres he received in Rawdon because of family illness, bought 300 acres in 1798, and shortly afterwards went to York (Toronto), where he obtained another grant. There was a shift to urban centres, and a move by ethnic groups to settle together: Irish from the Ninety-Six District of South Carolina moved to Rawdon; Germans settled at Ship Harbour, and Scots at Jordan River or Tusket. Over the years the settlers and their descendants tended to see themselves as Scots, Irishmen, Englishmen, Germans, and Africans rather than as Loyalists.

Although it is often said that the Loyalists brought to Nova Scotia a "bishopric, a college and a magazine", the Loyalist tradition was not as strong as it was in New Brunswick, where it founded a province.

P.R.B.

1. Morse's Report, 1784, D. Brymner, ed., *Report of the Public Archives for the year 1884* (Ottawa, 1885), p. xlii.

2. PANS, MG 12, misc. no. 4. Board of Accounts, 11 June 1784, refused to pay this. Small purchased an adjoining estate, which he called "Selma Hall."

3. PANS, MG 100, vol. 174, no. 36, W. Nesbitt to J. Leggett, 3 November 1783.

4. Parr to Shelburne, 24 January 1784, A.G. Doughty, ed., *Report of the Public Archives for the Year 1921* (Ottawa, 1922), Appendix E, p. 4.

5. PANS, MG 12, H.Q. 1, p. 128a, Orders, Halifax, 14 November 1783.

6. There were only nine women, five children, and ten servants in the settlement. "It was almost a womanless Eden," according to Dr. A.C. Jost in *Guysborough Sketches and Essays* (Guysborough, 1950), p. 120.

7. Parr to J. Wentworth, 5 March 1788, PRO, C.O. 217/61, *ff.* 55–56. Enclosed in Parr to Stanley, 29 December 1788. A.C. Jost, *Guysborough Sketches*, pp. 281–95, shows that about 25 men remained on their land for more than a decade, and almost all of them were married.

8. PANS, RG 1, vol. 376, pp. 1–21, J. Robinson to E. Winslow, 29 May 1784.

9. E.A. Jones, "The Loyalists of New Jersey," *Collections of New Jersey Historical Society*, vol. 10 (1927), pp. 143–45; C.B. Fergusson, ed., *A Directory of the Members of the Legislative Assembly of Nova Scotia, 1758–1958* (Halifax, 1958), pp. 250–51.

10. J. St. G. Walker, *The Black Loyalists: The Search for a Promised Land in Nova Scotia and Sierra Leone, 1783–1870* (New York and Halifax, 1976), p. 22.

11. B. Marston, Diary for Monday, July 26, 1784, University of New Brunswick Library, p. 265.

12. PANS, RG 1, vol. 376, pp. 29–30, J. Robinson to E. Winslow, 2 August 1784.

13. Stewart to Campbell, 25 June 1784, PANS, RG 1, vol. 376, pp. 78–81. Stewart threatened to stop the bounty from anyone who sold his ration. He had struck off Captain A. MacMillan, who had been court-martialled.

14. Parr to Nepean, Halifax, 11 October 1785, PRO., C.O. 217/57, *ff.* 155–58.

15. According to Margaret Ells' analysis from the land papers of the dispersion of American Loyalists in Nova Scotia from 1783 to 1800.

Between 1775 and 1784 about forty thousand Loyalist refugees left the rebellious American colonies and found sanctuary in British North America. The vast majority arrived in 1783 and 1784.

107. Travelling chest
Ca. 1780
Pine, leather covered with brass studding
L. 48.3 cm; W. 27.0 cm;
H. 28.0 cm

Mr. and Mrs. George Bruce, Shelburne, Nova Scotia

108. Purse
Joseph Rives
Liverpool, England
Ca. 1775
Leather
16.4 cm × 11.7 cm

Canadian War Museum, Ottawa
No. 1981-730/1

109. George III farthing
Great Britain
1773
Obverse, laureate head
Diam. 2.5 cm

New Brunswick Museum, Saint John

The crude minting of this coin suggests that it is possibly a contemporary counterfeit, many of which circulated in the colonies.

110. George III halfpenny
Great Britain
1773
Obverse, laureate head
Diam. 2.8 cm

New Brunswick Museum, Saint John

111. George III halfpenny
Great Britain
1775
Reverse, Britannia seated
Diam. 2.8 cm

New Brunswick Museum, Saint John

112. George Washington cent
United States of America
1783
Obverse, laureate head
Diam. 2.8 cm

New Brunswick Museum, Saint John

113. One-shilling note
New Jersey
1776
Obverse, no. 41176
10.8 cm × 6.0 cm

Mr. John Wentworth Moody, Ottawa

114. One-shilling note
New Jersey
1776
Reverse, no. 44362
10.8 cm × 6.0 cm

New Brunswick Museum, Saint
John

115. Two-shilling note
Counties of New-Castle, Kent
and Sussex, on Delaware
1759
Obverse, no. 2343
7.4 cm × 9.0 cm

Mr. John Wentworth Moody,
Ottawa

116. Three-shilling note
New Jersey
1776
Obverse, no. 46131
10.6 cm × 6.7 cm

Mr. John Wentworth Moody,
Ottawa

117. Fifteen-shilling note
Pennsylvania
1773
Obverse, no. 18612
7.0 cm × 9.9 cm

New Brunswick Museum, Saint
John

118. Thirty-dollar note
United Colonies
1777
Obverse
9.4 cm × 7.2 cm

New Brunswick Museum, Saint
John
No. 5687

In March 1776, the arrival of the fleet and army following the evacuation of Boston made Halifax temporarily the principal centre of British power in North America. This precipitate removal brought the first substantial group of Loyalists to Nova Scotia. Throughout the war, other Loyalists continued to trickle into the province, before the mass exodus from the rebel colonies in 1783.

119. Halifax, Nova Scotia, showing Fort Needham in the foreground and Halifax Citadel, Town, and Harbour in the background
Ca. 1776
Aquatint in sepia on paper, after a drawing by Lieutenant Colonel Edward Hicks
54.5 cm × 32.5 cm

New Brunswick Museum, Saint John
No. W. 668

The Bearer James Loveless, Loyalist—Having some Business to Settle at Halifax has Requested This Pass. He is victualled to 30th Inst.
[signed] Geo. Lawe
Super^t Loyalists
To Whom it may Concern

120. Pass issued to James Loveless, Loyalist
12 September 1785
30.0 cm × 18.7 cm

Public Archives of Nova Scotia, Halifax
Ref.: MG 100, vol. 178, no. 27

MacMillan, an eight-year veteran of the Royal Highland Emigrants, later the 84th Foot, settled in Nova Scotia after the war, as did the majority of his regiment's 2nd Battalion.

121. Discharge of Donald MacMillan, private soldier of the 84th Foot
1783
33.0 cm × 21.0 cm

Public Archives of Nova Scotia, Halifax
Ref.: MG 100, vol. 184, no. 22

The great majority of Loyalists who departed the American colonies by sea in 1783 came to Port Roseway. In July 1783 it was officially named Shelburne, in honour of the secretary of state for the colonies. Because of the great influx of temporary residents the early growth and rapid decline of Shelburne was remarkable. William Booth's drawing dates from shortly after the town peaked in 1786–1787.

122. Part of the town of Shelburne in Nova Scotia, with the barracks opposite
William Booth
1789
Wash drawing on paper
29.2 cm × 54.6 cm

Picture Division, Public Archives of Canada, Ottawa
No. C-10548

123. A Black woodcutter at Shelburne, Nova Scotia

William Booth
1788
Watercolour on paper
16.5 cm × 22.7 cm

Picture Division, Public Archives of Canada, Ottawa
No. 1970-188-1090

Black Loyalists dreamed of a new world of dignity, independence, and equal citizenship when they left the American colonies. About three thousand settled among their white counterparts in Nova Scotia; but their neighbours still saw them as inferiors, and the Blacks faced a new bondage to white whims and prejudices. They very soon began to settle in segregated communities, but even this did not solve their problems. In 1792 nearly twelve hundred Black Loyalists left the province for Sierra Leone.

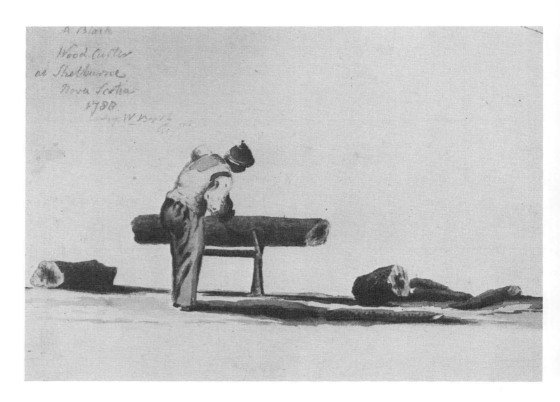

124. James Moody's commission as lieutenant colonel commandant of the militia of Clare Township, Annapolis County

1798
Paper
41.1 cm × 32.3 cm

Mr. John Wentworth Moody, Ottawa

New Jersey Volunteers veteran James Moody settled at Sissiboo (Weymouth), where he became a notable member of the community, engaged in farming and shipbuilding. Like most half-pay officers of the colonial rebellion, he also served in the local militia. He received a captain's commission in the Royal Nova Scotia Regiment and served throughout its nine-year existence (1793–1802). In 1798 he was given command of the Clare Township Battalion of the Nova Scotia militia. From 1793 to 1806 Moody represented Annapolis County, which included present-day Digby County, in the House of Assembly. He died at Weymouth in 1809.

125. Shoe buckles of James Moody
Probably English
Ca. 1780
Silver plate, enamel, and gloss
7.0 cm × 5.3 cm;
7.3 cm × 5.3 cm

Mr. John Wentworth Moody, Ottawa

During the period 1865–1875, Mrs. Susanna Lucy Anne Weldon (b. 1817, Windsor, Nova Scotia) collected porcelain and pottery belonging to the descendants of Loyalists and other early settlers in the Maritimes. The Weldon Collection was acquired by the University of King's College, Halifax.

This figure belonged to Captain Bailey of the Loyal American Regiment, who settled in Fredericton after the rebellion.

126. St. George and the dragon
Wood and Caldwell, Burslem, Staffordshire
1790–1818
English earthenware, painted in enamel colours with silver lustre
H. 27.0 cm; W. 18.5 cm

University of King's College, Halifax
No. W 125

This oval pierced drainer was designed to rest on a platter.

127. Serving dish owned by the family of Timothy Ruggles
Ca. 1780–1790
English pearlware
24.0 cm × 17.4 cm

University of King's College, Halifax
No. W 129.6

128. Cup belonging to Sir Guy Carleton

Ca. 1780
English porcelain, unmarked, with gilt rim and gilt bellflower motif on handle
H. 6.0 cm; Diam. 6.5 cm

University of King's College, Halifax
No. W 65

129. Dish belonging to Colonel Winckworth Tonge

Ca. 1790–1800
Chinese export porcelain, in Canton pattern
40.0 cm × 32.6 cm

University of King's College, Halifax
No. W 81h

After devoting his early adulthood to a military career in America, Winckworth Tonge came to Nova Scotia and acquired extensive lands that had belonged to exiled Acadians. At the start of the rebellion, he volunteered for service in the Nova Scotia militia. In 1781 he rose to the rank of colonel.

130. Sauceboat belonging to Amos Botsford

Ca. 1760
Chinese export porcelain, painted in famille-rose enamels
L. 19.0 cm; H. 6.7 cm; W. 10.3 cm

University of King's College, Halifax
No. W 88

Botsford, a Loyalist from Newtown, Connecticut, came to New Brunswick in 1784. He was the first speaker of the House of Assembly of the new province.

Loyalist Military Settlement in New Brunswick

by Wallace Brown

Professor of History
University of New Brunswick at Fredericton

During 1783 the old province of Nova Scotia received as many as thirty-five thousand Loyalists, and almost fifteen thousand settled north of Chignecto Bay. Loyalist army officers campaigned to partition the province, and in August 1784 New Brunswick was created. Unlike Nova Scotia, New Brunswick, with only about three thousand pre-Loyalists, half of whom were Acadians, plus a few hundred Malecite Indians, was virtually a wilderness. (Many Acadians suffered a second "dérangement" when, to make way for the Loyalists, they were forced to move north from the lower St. John River to Madawaska.) This Loyalist dominance persisted, for New Brunswick had little further immigration until after the War of 1812.[1]

About half the New Brunswick Loyalists were disbanded soldiers and their dependants, representing about twenty of the fifty provincial corps formed during the war. They were known as "provincials" to distinguish them from "civilian refugees", but the difference is not always clear. Some civilians had served in regiments, and others, such as the Associated Loyalists, had fought in non-regimental units.[2]

Apart from the Penobscot Loyalists who crossed Passamaquoddy Bay from what is now Maine, almost all New Brunswick Loyalists, both refugees and provincials, were evacuated at government expense from New York and environs to the mouth of the St. John River. The Spring Fleet disembarked on May 18, and this remains the official anniversary commemorating the Loyalist landing in the province. There was also a June Fleet, and a Fall Fleet that arrived in September and was largely made up of provincials under the command of Colonel Richard Hewlett. Smaller numbers of provincials arrived throughout the year.[3]

The voyage lasted only a few days, but it was never pleasant and, in one case, proved fatal. The *Martha* foundered near the entrance to the Bay of Fundy, and many provincials from the Maryland Loyalists and the 2nd DeLancey's were lost.

Overwhelmed by his task and reluctant to promote a rival settlement, Nova Scotia Governor John Parr had done little to prepare the hamlets at the mouth of the St. John River for the large number of immigrants. Because transportation upstream was scarce and the land was not generally ready for settlement, most Loyalists spent the winter around Carleton and Parrtown (Saint John). They huddled in spruce-covered tents and makeshift huts, exposed to bitter cold and suffering from lack of food. Quarrelling and drunkenness were common, and deaths all too frequent.[4]

In the spring of 1784, the Loyalists began to claim their land. The largest number settled along the St. John River as far north as Woodstock. They fanned out along its bays and the shores of Grand Lake, and along several tributaries, notably the Kennebecasis and the Nashwaak. The second most important area of settlement was Passamaquoddy Bay, particularly St. Andrews, and the St. Croix estuary in the St. Stephen region. Smaller settlements sprang up along the Bay of Fundy, the Petitcodiac River, the Vale of Sussex, the Miramichi, the Bay of Chaleur, and at Sackville.

Small numbers of the King's Orange Rangers settled the Quaco-St. Martins area east of Saint John; a few Nova Scotians of the Royal Fencible Americans, which had garrisoned Fort Howe when the fleets arrived, settled at St. George; many Scots of the North Carolina Volunteers joined their countrymen on the Miramichi; and some Westchester Loyalists settled near Fort Cumberland (Beauséjour).

Although pockets of provincials could be found virtually everywhere, most were assigned land in the St. John valley upstream from Fredericton. This region had been designated on the basis of favourable military surveys, and in order to strengthen communications between Québec and Halifax. Fourteen blocks were surveyed and drawn by lot by the commanding officers, but only the first eight, as far as Woodstock, were settled.[5]

Most provincials had been recruited in the Middle Colonies and in the colonial South, but many had originated in New England. The King's American Dragoons, for example, under the command of Benjamin Thompson (later Count Rumford) were composed of a number of New Englanders. More than 350 dragoons arrived with the Spring Fleet. In September they were ordered to the Pokiok River, the first provincial settlers to be sent upstream. They received land between Long's Creek and the Pokiok, and the parish was named Prince William after the regiment's patron. Noteworthy ex-dragoons included Major Joshua Upham, a judge of the Supreme Court and member of the council; Major Daniel Murray, an assembly member; Dr. Adino Paddock, a distinguished

Saint John physician; and the regiment's chaplain, Reverend Jonathan Odell, a leading versifier and longtime provincial secretary.[6]

Many New York Volunteers settled the upper valley of the Keswick. In 1776 the regiment had helped capture Long Island, and had taken part in the defence of Savannah in 1779, in the capture of Charleston and in the battle of Camden in 1780. The regiment's Major John Coffin had launched the battle that resulted in the British victory at Eutaw Springs in 1781. Major Coffin built Alwington Manor at Nerepis, Kings County, and served in the New Brunswick House of Assembly and on the Executive Council.[7]

DeLancey's Brigade had also seen distinguished service. Oliver DeLancey, scion of a great colonial New York family, became the senior Loyalist officer. His 2nd Battalion was noted for its part in the defence of Ninety-Six, South Carolina, in 1781. The 1st and 2nd Battalions settled in the parish of Woodstock. In the fall of 1783 the 3rd Battalion, commanded by Lieutenant Colonel Richard Hewlett, settled well south of Fredericton. Hampstead, Queens County, was named after Hewlett's Long Island home. Gabriel G. Ludlow, colonel of the 2nd Battalion, became the first mayor of Saint John and, after Governor Thomas Carleton's return to England, president of the council and effective head of the New Brunswick government.

The New Jersey Volunteers, which included many New Yorkers, were also known as Skinner's Cowboys because of General Cortlandt Skinner's guerrilla activities around Philadelphia. Many of the volunteers were led by Lieutenant Colonel Isaac Allen to the Kingsclear area; others settled on the Kennebecasis. The New Jersey Volunteers contributed many leading citizens to New Brunswick, including Dr. Charles Earle, a prominent Fredericton doctor, and Ensign Xenophon Lovett, who served as usher of the Black Rod for almost fifty years. When Chaplain Charles Inglis became the first bishop of Nova Scotia, his bishopric included New Brunswick.[8]

The Loyal American Regiment was raised by Colonel Beverley Robinson, a native of New York. The regiment fought in New York and Pennsylvania, and suffered severe losses at the battle of King's Mountain on the border of the Carolinas in 1780. After the war, most of the corps went to Nova Scotia, but some settled along the St. John River. The colonel's son

John became a mayor of Saint John and the first president of the Bank of New Brunswick. The regiment's chaplain, John Beardsley, became rector of Maugerville; surgeon Peter Huggeford, an outstanding Saint John doctor; and Lieutenant John Ward, a successful merchant and pioneer of steamboat travel between Saint John and Fredericton.[9]

Raised in New York, the King's American Regiment clashed with the rebels in New York, in Connecticut, and in the South. Veterans of the regiment settled from the Pokiok to the Eel River, west of the lands granted to the King's American Dragoons. Captain Abraham dePeyster of Maugerville, who became treasurer of the province, and Ensign Henry Nase, a leading magistrate and citizen of Westfield, had both served with the King's American Regiment.[10]

No Loyalist corps was more celebrated than the Queen's Rangers. Colonel Robert Rogers, who commanded the famous Rogers' Rangers during the Seven Years' War, recruited the regiment in 1776 mainly in New York and Connecticut (later the Queen's Own Loyal Virginia Regiment joined the unit). In 1777, despite many casualties, the Queen's Rangers helped defeat Washington at Brandywine Creek. After Brandywine, Lieutenant Colonel John Graves Simcoe assumed command, and the regiment distinguished itself throughout the southern campaigns in 1780 and 1781. Among those injured at Brandywine Creek were Captain John Saunders, a Virginian, who became chief justice of New Brunswick, and another Virginian, Lieutenant Stair Agnew, who sat in the assembly for many years. Although some of the veterans took up land in the St. George area, most settled in York County and gave their regiment's name to the parish of Queensbury.[11]

The Prince of Wales American Regiment is best known for its engagement of General Thomas Sumter at Hanging Rock, South Carolina. The regiment settled on the Keswick River and south of its confluence with the St. John. Lieutenant Munson Hoyt became a Fredericton pioneer, and Captain Daniel Lyman an early member of the assembly for York County.

The Loyal American Legion was commanded by Benedict Arnold who, whatever his faults, was one of the ablest generals of the war. He lived for a time in Fredericton and St. John.[12]

One of the few instances of Black Loyalist immigration was the group of eighty-nine Black

Pioneers of the Royal Guides attached to the Loyal American Regiment. Both Pioneers and Guides settled along the Saint John River above the Keswick. Many soldiers of the Pennsylvania Loyalist Regiment settled across the river from DeLancey's men; the surviving Maryland Loyalists settled near Fredericton.

However, the military Loyalists did not usually settle in the neatly laid-out areas assigned to them. Such was the preference for land near Saint John that Brigadier General Henry Fox, the commanding officer in Halifax, had to order the troops northwards. It is estimated that fewer than one man in ten actually went to his assigned land, and even fewer remained there.

Many Loyalists moved within the province, and about fifteen per cent left New Brunswick, mainly for the United States and Upper Canada. Settlers on rich intervale lands tended to stay put, but those on poor land, such as members of the New Jersey Volunteers and the Loyal American Regiment, caught "Niagara fever" and left Grand Lake, the Miramichi, and the Penniac in response to tempting offers of fertile, free land by John Graves Simcoe, the first lieutenant governor of Upper Canada.[13]

The New Brunswick provincials, like most Loyalists, faced "that permanent North American war, the war against the wilderness". They received standard government aid: free land on the usual scale, and food, seed, tools, clothing, and other supplies for three years. Officers got half-pay, and all soldiers retained their arms and accoutrements; a few received compensation for losses suffered during the war, and fewer still gained government office.

Opinions vary regarding their quality as pioneers. Some half-pay officers, partly because of their secure income, were deemed particularly successful farmers. Some observers praised the cohesion of the former military units. Others, however, found that "vice of every kind, incident of the camp . . . prevailed", and bemoaned the "rum and idle habits contracted during the war".[14]

Whether good or poor farmers, the provincials often had little choice of occupation. For example, Azor Betts, a former surgeon with the Queen's Rangers, was forced to farm because he could find few paying patients. Lord Edward Fitzgerald rather exaggerated the frontier as social equalizer when he wrote: "There are no gentlemen; everyman is on a footing (provided he works) and wants nothing; every man is ex-

actly what he can make himself." Yet there was a good deal of truth in what he said. John Saunders' dream of a great landed estate, "the Barony" at Prince William, failed for lack of tenants. In the 1780s William Cobbett was amazed to find "thousands of captains . . . without shoes, and squires without stockings", some of whom were happy to sell him a glass of grog. Later an English visitor was astonished to find John Coffin, then a general, "retailing cabbages" at the Market Slip in Saint John.[15]

The provincials played a large rôle in most aspects of early New Brunswick history and enjoyed the modest agricultural prosperity described by Edward Winslow in 1802. Generally, however, we cannot discuss them *qua* provincials except in their rôle in the militia and their initial relationship with Lieutenant Governor Thomas Carleton.

The provincials were the backbone of the militia. During the war scare with France in 1793 and with the United States in 1808, they turned out in enthusiastic, embarrassingly large numbers. When war finally did come in 1812, however, the concentration of operations in Upper Canada denied any test to the New Brunswick militia.

Carleton had been a professional soldier, and as lieutenant governor he surrounded himself with provincial army officers. He chose St. Anne's Point as the provincial capital in 1784 because of the large population of ex-officers and non-commissioned officers, which gave the area a rural, military atmosphere. Fittingly, the new town was named Fredericton after George III's second son, renowned as a patron of the army. Among those provincials who worked with Carleton were Colonel Gabriel G. Ludlow as senior councillor; Johathan Odell as secretary; Captain Isaac Allen and Major Joshua Upham of the King's American Dragoons as Supreme Court judges; Captain John Coffin, Colonel Beverley Robinson, Jr., and Major Gilfred Studholm of the Royal Fencible Americans as councillors.[16]

The lieutenant governor also relied on men who had worked with the army, particularly in New York under his brother Guy. Among them were George D. Ludlow, former supervisor of police on Long Island, who became chief justice; George Leonard of the Associated Refugees, Abijah Willard of the commissary general's department, and Edward Winslow, a former muster-master general, all of whom became councillors; James Putnam of the barrack-master general's department, later Supreme Court judge; and Ward Chipman, who became Winslow's deputy.[17]

Initially, the two greatest concentrations of Loyalists in British North America were in Shelburne, Nova Scotia, and the St. John River valley. While the former failed dismally, the latter succeeded. The two greatest concentrations of provincials were in Upper Canada and the St. John valley; both were successful.

W.B.

1. W.S. McNutt, *New Brunswick, A History 1784-1867* (Toronto, 1963), chapters 2 and 3; E.C. Wright, *The Loyalists of New Brunswick* (Fredericton, 1955), *passim*.

2. McNutt, *New Brunswick*, pp. 22-41; Wright, *Loyalists of N.B.*, pp. 151-53.

3. *Ibid.*, chapter 4; McNutt, *New Brunswick*, chapter 2.

4. Wright, *Loyalists of N.B.*, pp. 86-87; McNutt, *New Brunswick*, pp. 26-27; P. Fisher, *History of New Brunswick* (Saint John, 1825; reprinted 1921), pp. 11-13.

5. W.O. Raymond, "Loyalists in Arms," *New Brunswick Historical Society Collections*, no. 5 (1904), pp. 189-223; Wright, *Loyalists of N.B.*, chapter 9.

6. McNutt, *New Brunswick*, pp. 13-25; Raymond, "Loyalists in Arms," pp. 211-12.

7. *Ibid.*, pp. 199-200; McNutt, *New Brunswick*, p. 25.

8. Raymond, "Loyalists in Arms," pp. 207-9 and 212-17; McNutt, *New Brunswick*, p. 31.

9. Raymond, "Loyalists in Arms," pp. 206-7 and 211.

10. *Ibid.*, pp. 203-4.

11. *Ibid.*, pp. 202-3.

12. *Ibid.*, pp. 193 and 209-11.

13. Wright, *Loyalists of N.B.*, pp. 212-15.

14. R. Fellows, "The Loyalists and Land Settlement in New Brunswick, 1783-1790," Canadian Archivist, vol. 2 (1971), pp. 5-15; W.O. Raymond, ed., *The Winslow Papers* (Saint John, 1901), p. 337.

15. PRO, A.O. (Audit Office) 13/11, quoted in Wright, *Loyalists of N.B.*, p. 220; quoted in W. Brown, "William Cobbett in the Maritimes," *Dalhousie Review*, vol. 56 (1976), p. 452; H. Temperley, ed., *Gubbins' New Brunswick Journal, 1811 and 1813* (Fredericton, 1980), p. 84.

16. Raymond, ed., *Winslow Papers*, pp. 468-72; McNutt, *New Brunswick*, pp. 57 and 133.

17. *Ibid.*, pp. 48-53.

131. General Thomas Carleton

Sampson Towgood Roche
(*attrib.*)
English
Ca. 1795
Watercolour on ivory
5.9 cm × 4.6 cm oval

Beaverbrook Art Gallery,
Fredericton, gift of Lord
Dorchester, 1963
No. 63.26

Thomas Carleton, the younger brother of Sir Guy Carleton, served as quarter-master general at Québec during the American rebellion. In 1784 he became lieutenant governor of New Brunswick, an appointment he later described as "one of the most fortunate events of my life".

Carleton apparently was in accord with the New Brunswick Loyalist élite, and this close cooperation profoundly influenced the shape of the new province in spite of the elected Assembly's suggestions of incompetence and misrule. In the face of years of what Carleton called the "usages of the late New England provinces", he left New Brunswick for England in October 1803. However, he remained lieutenant governor and a supporter of New Brunswick interests until his death in 1817. Despite the fact that he lived in England for the last fourteen years of his term, Thomas Carleton was the key figure among the founding fathers of New Brunswick.

132. Campaign Table

New Brunswick
1812 period
Mahogany, pine secondary
75.9 cm × 85.8 cm (leaves
extended); H. 77.0 cm

New Brunswick Museum, Saint
John
No. 61.88

This portable campaign table was used by General John Coffin during the War of 1812. It served as a toilet table, dining table, and work table in the field. The top lifts to reveal pewter dishes and storage compartments. The legs are removable and can be stored in a compartment at the right side of the table.

A native of Boston, John Coffin worked as a sea captain until rebellion broke out in the colonies. He joined the British Army at the Battle of Bunker Hill, where he gained the rank of ensign. By the end of the war he had attained the rank of major.

After the war, he moved to New Brunswick and acquired 6000 acres of land at the mouth of the Nerepis River in Kings County. When the United States threatened the security of New Brunswick in 1812, Coffin raised four hundred men for military service. He eventually became a general.

John Murray (1720–1794) was a leading citizen and politician of Massachusetts before the rebellion. During the Seven Years' War, he achieved the rank of colonel in the Massachusetts militia. He was an active supporter of the Crown, and for this reason a rebel mob forcibly entered his home in 1776. Though Murray himself was absent, the visitors left their message by piercing the head of his portrait by J.S. Copley.

Murray emigrated to Wales, living in poverty until after the war. He then moved to Saint John, where he purchased property and enjoyed a prosperous life.

133. Colonel John Murray
John Singleton Copley
American
1762
Oil on canvas
124.4 cm × 99.0 cm

New Brunswick Museum, Saint John
No. 59.60

134. Waistcoat belonging to Colonel John Murray
4th quarter 18th century
Silk satin, blue, with sequinned metallic lace

New Brunswick Museum, Saint John
No. 59.80

135. Cutlery chest belonging to Colonel John Murray
1760s
Leather over pine, brass furniture
H. 31.2 cm; W. 22.7 cm; Depth 20.0 cm

New Brunswick Museum, Saint John
No. 59.74

136. Knife from Colonel John Murray's cutlery
William Abdy, London
1767
Silver
L. 27.5 cm

New Brunswick Museum, Saint John
No. 59.74

137. Fork from Colonel John Murray's cutlery
William Abdy, London
1767
Silver
L. 22.0 cm

New Brunswick Museum, Saint John
No. 59.74

138. Spoon from Colonel John Murray's cutlery
T. and N. Chawner, London
1765
L. 20.2 cm

New Brunswick Museum, Saint John
No. 59.74

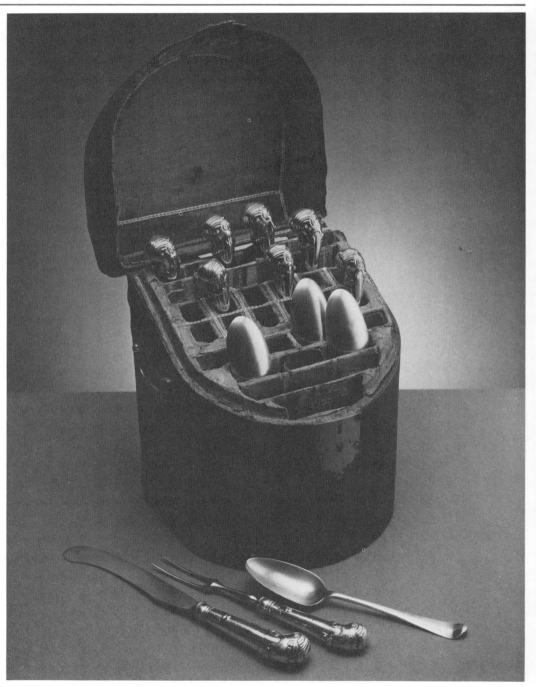

The coat of arms of this cup is probably "adoptive", as no Deveber family is known to have been granted arms. It was not uncommon for persons of some means to adopt arms of their own invention and to have their silver engraved with them. This may have been done by Deveber himself or by an ancestor. If the latter, the family of Gabriel Deveber may have simply "inherited" the arms without being aware of their questionable origin.

139. Cup belonging to Gabriel Deveber
Samuel Courtauld, Sr.
England
1750–1751
Silver
H. 9.3 cm; Diam. at base 7.1 cm

New Brunswick Museum, Saint John
No. 54.136

140. Colonel Beverley Robinson
Hand-coloured photograph of a portrait by Matthew Pratt
10.0 cm × 8.0 cm

New Brunswick Museum, Saint John
No. W. 1492

A wealthy landowner in New York State before the rebellion, Beverley Robinson (1723–1792) raised the Loyal American Regiment primarily from among his tenants. He commanded his regiment throughout the war. Since he moved to England when hostilities ended, the table probably came to New Brunswick with one of his two sons who settled there.

141. Drop-leaf pedestal table
Colonel Beverley Robinson (*attrib.*)
Top of bird's eye maple, on tripod pedestal
38.1 cm × 27.9 cm oval; H. 54.5 cm

New Brunswick Museum, Saint John
No. 69.89

John Robinson (1762–1828), son of Colonel Beverley Robinson, secured his commission as lieutenant in his father's Loyal American Regiment. After the rebellion, Robinson became a successful businessman and politician in Saint John.

142. John Robinson
H.C. Pratt
1826
Oil on canvas
75.0 cm × 62.0 cm

New Brunswick Museum, Saint John
No. 62.129

143. Hepplewhite armchair belonging to Benedict Arnold
H. 93.5 cm; W. 58.0 cm; Depth 58.0 cm

New Brunswick Museum, Saint John
No. 47.12

At the end of hostilities Benedict Arnold managed to escape to England, where he received compensation for his losses. He returned to North America and settled in Saint John. There, from 1785 to 1791, he engaged none too successfully in trade. When he left New Brunswick in 1791, following a fire at his place of business, he sold his possessions by public auction. This chair was from his residence in Saint John.

144. Personal letter seal and ivory handle of Reverend Jonathan Odell
H. 1.7 cm; Diam. 3.9 cm; L. of ivory handle 8.6 cm

New Brunswick Museum, Saint John
No. 30094

Jonathan Odell (1737–1818) of Newark, New Jersey, entered the medical profession and served for a time as surgeon in the British Army. He then was ordained and appointed rector in Burlington, New Jersey. During the rebellion Odell was chaplain to the Pennsylvania Loyalists and, later, to the King's American Dragoons. He also served briefly as secretary to Sir Guy Carleton.

In 1784 Odell settled his family in New Brunswick, where he held a number of lucrative government appointments. He is chiefly remembered as provincial secretary of the infant province. He died at Fredericton.

Loyalist Military Settlement in Québec
by Robert S. Allen

Immediately following the outbreak of civil war and rebellion in colonial America in April 1775, Loyalists from upper New York and the backwoods of New England began trekking to Québec. Most of these loyal refugees who abandoned their farms and followed the Lake Champlain route to Québec were Scotch Highlanders, German Palatines, and Quakers.

A significant number of Loyalist families entered Québec unnoticed or unrecorded, and quietly established themselves throughout the province. Others, however, were funnelled through Loyalist refugee camps established to accommodate destitute families, principally at Sorel and Machiche in the Lac Saint-Pierre area.[1] Other temporary settlements were located around Montreal and along the Richelieu River, notably at St. John's (Saint-Jean). In the camps, barracks, houses, and schools were built, and clothing, provisions, and tools were provided from the King's stores.[2] As the population was transient, enumeration was difficult. But a "Return of Loyalists in Canada" taken in March 1783 lists nearly two thousand individuals and families receiving provisions from His Majesty's government.[3]

The newly arrived Loyalists organized several independent companies and provincial corps.[4] For these units, the American rebellion was also a fiercely partisan civil war, as evidenced by the savage and stubborn intensity of the combatants at the battles of Oriskany and Bennington. The Royal Highland Emigrants, the King's Royal Regiment of New York, Butler's Rangers, the King's Rangers, the King's Loyal Americans, and the Queen's Loyal Rangers served in the northern campaign and contributed to the military defence and security of Quebec.

Much of the success of these corps was due to the organizational abilities and determination of their leaders, pre-eminent among whom was Sir John Johnson (1742–1830). Born in the Mohawk Valley of upper New York, Sir John was the son and heir to the massive estates of Sir William Johnson. When the rebellion broke out, Johnson moved to the Montreal area and convinced several hundred other subjects, particularly the Highland tenants of his estates, to join the royal standard. He raised and commanded the two battalions of the King's Royal Regiment of New York, the largest provincial corps in Québec, and conducted raids into the back settlements of New York, often against his rebel neighbours.

In March 1782 Johnson became Superintendent General and Inspector General of Indian Affairs, a position he held until 1828.[5] He was appointed to the legislative council of Québec in 1787 and to the legislative council of Lower Canada in 1796. During the War of 1812, he commanded the Six Township battalions of Québec militia. One of Johnson's major accomplishments was the successful resetting of the Loyalists, especially along the upper St. Lawrence.[6]

The Loyalist provincial corps disbanded in 1783 and 1784. In the late spring of 1784 most of these ex-soldiers and their families set sail for the upper St. Lawrence and the Bay of Quinté, where they established new settlements. Others went to Cape Breton Island,[7] and a "Return of Loyalist and Discharged Soldiers, Embarked on Boarde the Provinces Vessels fore Chaleur Bay" shows that about four hundred men, women, and children were settled in the Gaspé.[8] An undetermined number of Loyalist families settled elsewhere in the province, notably in the towns along the Richelieu River and at Montreal and Québec.

One group of loyal Americans demonstrated an "indecent perseverance" in establishing settlements in the Missisquoi Bay area, north of Lake Champlain, contrary to the policy of Frederick Haldimand, Governor of Québec.[9] During the war, the provincial corps had continually travelled through the region on scouting and foraging expeditions. The Loyalists were well aware that this unoccupied and partially cleared area was potentially rich farmland. Easy water transportation to the towns along the Richelieu River and lower Lake Champlain assured access to a market for agricultural products. These prospects prompted some men to petition on behalf of themselves and the Associated Loyalists for land grants around Missisquoi Bay. Haldimand, however, remained adamant that "the Frontier to the east of the St. Lawrence should be left unsettled for some time, and then [settled] by French Canadians", who regarded the area as part of their natural heritage.[10] Settling the Loyalists so close to the border and their recent enemies was also deemed unwise. It was suspected that certain Loyalists wished to settle there to conduct an illicit trade or "paltry traffic" with the Americans.[11] For these reasons, all Loyalist petitions for land grants in the Missisquoi Bay area were rejected.

John Walden Meyers (1745–1821), who had carried secret despatches between New York and Québec during the Revolutionary War, was one of the Loyalists who petitioned to settle in the Missisquoi Bay area.[12] Meyers led the group of Associated Loyalists who sent the first formal petition to Haldimand. Although Meyers eventually moved to the Bay of Quinté, his efforts encouraged many other Loyalists to remain in what became Missisquoi County and the Eastern Townships.

John Peters (1740–1788) was another Loyalist who tried unsuccessfully to defy Haldimand. Peters had organized and commanded the Queen's Loyal Rangers, who were decimated at Bennington in August 1777 during the Burgoyne campaign. He was subsequently appointed a "Captain of Invalides" in the Loyal Rangers, which he regarded as a "cruel degrading change". Peters believed that he was unfairly treated by Haldimand, and he developed a bitter animosity towards that "petty tyrant". He vehemently opposed the settlement of Loyalists in "so remote a place as Cataraqui (Kingston)", and vociferously supported those Loyalists at Missisquoi Bay who had defied the governor. Not surprisingly, Peters was unable to obtain a land grant, and moved first to Cape Breton Island and then to England.[13]

Despite these setbacks, most of the Loyalists at Missisquoi Bay persisted, declaring that "nothing but Superior force shall drive them off that land".[14] This impudence incensed Haldimand, who threatened to withdraw government provisions and burn the settlers' homes. He announced that he would not "upon any account whatever, grant a single acre of the Crown Land in that quarter, nor permit any person whosoever to settle there".[15]

There were rare exceptions to this policy. John Fordyce of New Hampshire, for example, received an early government grant. But most Missisquoi Bay settlers, faced with increasing economic hardships and stout government opposition, accepted a compromise. They became tenant farmers on three seigneuries of the region—Foucault, Noyan, and Saint-Armand. In 1789 the Honourable Thomas Dunn became the proprietor of the seigneury of Saint-Armand; thereafter he sold 200-acre lots to the Loyalists for about £20 each.[16] Today most of Foucault seigneury, later renamed Caldwell Manor, is in Vermont, but the character of Noyan and especially of Saint-Armand has been influenced by Loyalist settlers.

Typical of those settlers who through dogged determination became entrenched in the Missisquoi Bay area were Christian Wehr (1732–1824), Peter Miller (1740–1819), the brothers John (ca. 1740–1797) and Henry (ca. 1742–1819) Ruiter, and John Dewar (ca. 1745–1820). Wehr was born in the German Palatinate and emigrated to Albany County, New York, where he settled as a farmer at Claverack. Serving as a captain in the King's Loyal Americans, and then in the 2nd Battalion of the King's Royal Regiment of New York, he was appointed a lieutenant in 1781. In a "Return of Officers" compiled towards the end of the rebellion, he is listed as a "foreigner" with seven years of service.[17]

Christian Wehr was blessed with an eloquent literary style. His detailed memorials, petitioning for lands "East of Missique Bay" for the Loyalists, disputed the contention that the Loyalists there would engage in "trafficing" or "quarrelling with our nighbors", the Americans. Of the more than three hundred Loyalists in the area, Wehr explained, "the most General Part have been well liveing Farmers, and sons of able farmers, before the Rebellion in America, and those People who were brought up to cultivate the ground, have no other way, nither do they desire any other ways to maintain themselves and families, than by cultivation". Wehr advocated a humane policy that would allow the Loyalists to settle and farm peacefully on the desired lands, and enjoy "the Greater half of their Happiness in this world".[18] In spite of initial problems, Wehr's efforts were successful, and he lived and farmed for years on the lands of Saint-Armand. He was buried in the Methodist church cemetery plot marked "for soldiers" at Philipsburg, a new village whose founding was one product of the Loyalist settlement in the area.

Like Wehr, Peter Miller and the Ruiter brothers were of German Palatine origin and settled in Albany County, New York. After military service in the rebellion, they farmed in Missisquoi. Miller[19] and John Ruiter settled at Saint-Armand, where the latter was resident agent for Thomas Dunn. Henry Ruiter settled at Caldwell Manor and was one of the earliest to receive grants in Potton Township in 1799.[20] Dewar left Perth, Scotland, and arrived in New York about 1768. During the rebellion, he served as a "common soldier" in the King's Royal Regiment of New York. After the war, he joined the group of Loyalists who settled at Caldwell Manor where he was active in the burgeoning community life. He served in the War of 1812 as a captain of local militia and assisted later in the construction of the first Presbyterian church in the area.[21]

Some of the Loyalists of Missisquoi Bay fanned out through the surrounding countryside when the lands were opened for settlement in 1792, and the first township grants were made in 1796. Within Missisquoi County, there were thirty-five land grants in Dunham Township by 1796, and forty-five grants in Farnham Township by 1798.[22] Most of these grants were made to Loyalists. Nicholas Austin, a Quaker from New Hampshire, and Asa Porter from New York were among the first settlers of Bolton and Brome townships in Brome County. They were soon followed by other loyal Americans, and the permanent settlement of the Eastern Townships began.

Although the Quebec Loyalists included several ethnic and religious backgrounds, in time they came to be identified as the English-speaking community. While they retained a firm belief in the unity of the empire and the wisdom of British political institutions, they also contributed to the cultural richness of the province as their distinctive costume, food, music, and architectural design eventually blended with the traditions of Québec.

Missisquoi County today is a predominantly Francophone community, as Haldimand originally intended. Yet the towns of Clarenceville, Bedford, Saint-Armand, Frelighsburg, and Philipsburg still retain fine examples of Loyalist-era architecture. The Sir John Johnson Centennial Branch, the Heritage Branch of the United Empire Loyalists' Association of Canada, and the Missisquoi County Historical Society and Museum in Standbridge East are active in promoting a better understanding and appreciation of the Loyalist contribution to Canada. However, sensitive to the difficulties of defining loyalism in contemporary Québec and acutely aware of the change in the character of the population of the region, these associations possess a twinge of the *laager* mentality.

Nonetheless, the rôle of the Loyalists in what is now Québec and the impact of their settlement on the subsequent evolution of British North America were significant. It was the Loyalist provincial corps that were largely responsible for the successful military defence of the "old" province of Québec throughout the American rebellion (especially in 1775–1776 and following the Burgoyne campaign of 1777 when they provided garrison troops). This achievement preserved both the province and the French language and culture. This victory for "survivance", closely followed by the establishment of Loyalist settlements in the "old" provinces of Québec and Nova Scotia, created an ethnic and cultural duality that developed into the political concept of a federalism based on the principle of two "founding races". Although the positive and negative aspects of the concept can be argued, one cannot deny the profound importance of the settlement of the loyal Americans and their unique contribution to the political and cultural composition of Québec and Canada.

R.S.A.

1. W.H. Siebert, "The Temporary Settlement of Loyalists at Machiche, P.Q.," *Proceedings and Transactions of the Royal Society of Canada*, Third Series, vol. 8 (1914), Transactions, section 2, pp. 407–14.

2. *Ibid.*; and W.H. Siebert, "The American Loyalists in the Eastern Seigniories and Townships of the Province of Quebec," *Proceedings and Transactions of the Royal Society of Canada*, Third Series, vol. 7 (1913), Transactions, section 2, pp. 17, 18, 20, 27, 29, 30, and 31.

3. "Return of Loyalists in Canada, 1778–87," PAC, MG 21, Haldimand Collection, B116, March 1783.

4. M.B. Fryer, *King's Men: the Soldier-Founders of Ontario* (Toronto, 1980); for a specific example of independent Loyalist military activity, John M'Alpine, *Genuine Narratives and Concise Memoirs . . .* (Greenock, Scotland, 1780).

5. Commission dated 14 March 1782, PAC, MG 21, Haldimand Collection, B116.

6. Source material on Sir John Johnson is scattered throughout the Haldimand Collection and in his personal papers at the McLennan Library, McGill University. See also M.G. Walker, "Sir John Johnson, Loyalist," *Mississippi Valley Historical Review*, vol. 3 (1916), pp. 318–46.

7. Lists, with remarks, between 9 June and 8 November, 1784, PAC, MG 21, Haldimand Collection, B168.

8. For individual examples see Jonathan Jones in the Jones Family Papers, Collection 542, Queen's University Archives; The John Peters Narrative, Metropolitan Toronto Library.

9. Postscript to T.C. Lampee, ''The Missisquoi Loyalists,'' *Proceedings of the Vermont Historical Society*, vol. 6 (1938), p. 140.

10. Haldimand to Lord North, Quebec, August 1783, D. Brymer, ed., *Report of the Public Archives for the Year 1885* (Ottawa, 1886), p. 355; A.L. Burt, *The Old Province of Quebec* (republished Toronto, 1968), vol. 2, p. 86.

11. Lampee, ''Missisquoi Loyalists,'' p. 114. During the rebellion, smuggling in the Lake Champlain area was not uncommon. One notable example was Captain Azariah Pritchard of the King's Rangers and the British secret service, who traded with the enemy in beef.

12 Petition of 30 August 1783, *ibid.*, p. 111. For details on Meyers see *ibid.*, p. 112; M.B. Fryer, *Loyalist Spy* (Kingston, 1974); A. Fraser, ''United Empire Loyalists: Enquiry into the Losses and Services in Consequence of their Loyalty,'' *Second Report of the Bureau of Archives for the Province of Ontario, 1904* (Toronto, 1905), p. 1050 (hereafter ''Loyalist Claims'').

13. The John Peters Narrative.

14. Justice Sherwood to Major R. Mathews, St. John's (St-Jean), 1 March 1784, PAC, MG 21, Haldimand Collection, B162.

15. ''Letter to Major [J.] Campbell ordering him to remove settlers from Missisquoi Bay,'' 6 May 1784, PAC, RG 8, British Military and Naval Records, C Series, F13.

16. Lampee, ''Missisquoi Loyalists,'' p. 126.

17. *Ibid.*, pp. 135–36.

18. PAC, MG 21, Haldimand Collection, B167. For details see Lampee, ''Missisquoi Loyalists,'' pp. 117–19; A.M. McCaw, ''Christian Wehr, Portrait of a Pioneer,'' *The Loyalist Gazette* (1977), pp. 7–8.

19. See ''Loyalist Claims,'' pp. 407–8; Lampee, ''Missisquoi Loyalists,'' pp. 81–91, and 135; R.G. Moore, ''Peter Miller, Missisquoi Loyalist,'' *The Loyalist Gazette* (1970), p. 9.

20. See PAC, MG 23, G 111 3, ''Family Papers of John and Henry Ruiter of Missisquoi County, 1776–1835''; Lampee, ''Missisquoi Loyalists,'' pp. 120, 122, and 134; ''Loyalist Claims,'' pp. 941–42.

21. See *Missisquoi County Historical Society, Eighth Historical Report* (Stanbridge East, Quebec, 1965), pp. 122–29.

22. J.C. Langelier, comp., *List of Lands Granted by the Crown in the Province of Quebec from 1763 to 1890* (Quebec, 1891), pp. 616–26.

145. Sir Frederick Haldimand

Photographic reproduction of a painting from the studio of Sir Joshua Reynolds

Courtesy Alexander Raydon Gallery, New York

Frederick Haldimand (1718–1791) was a tough-minded but sensitive soldier-administrator of Swiss origin who rose to command a battalion of the Royal Americans (62nd, later 60th, Foot). In America during the Seven Years' War, he served at Carillon in 1758, at Oswego in 1759, and at the capitulation of Montreal in 1760. Haldimand remained in Canada until 1765.

In 1778 he returned to Québec, succeeding Sir Guy Carleton as governor of the province. His main concern until 1783 was strengthening Québec's military defence and dispatching raiding parties against American rebel back settlements.

At the end of the war, Haldimand turned his attention to the resettlement of the loyal Americans and the Mohawk Loyalists in British North America. His most delicate endeavour was to reconcile the Mohawk Loyalists to the loss of their ancestral lands. No less trying was the resettlement of seven thousand loyal Americans who flooded into Québec during the war. About one thousand settled in the province —in the Gaspé region, in the Eastern Townships, in towns along the Richelieu, and at Montréal and Québec. Provision was made for the remainder to go to areas along the upper St. Lawrence.

It was perhaps Haldimand's greatest contribution to muster, move, and settle the loyalist families in their military units. He wrote of the hard-won "mutual loyalties of comrades in war" as too valuable an asset "to throw away in the days of peace". In 1786 he was succeeded by Sir Guy Carleton (Lord Dorchester). Haldimand died in Switzerland in 1791.

The Royal Bounty of Provisions and Necessities

When the Loyalists moved to British North America, they were entitled to Royal Bounty. This included clothing, supplies, and tools from the King's stores, and substantially assisted the Loyalists in rebuilding their lives during their first years of settlement.

146. List of "Articles Wanted for the Loyalists in the Province of Quebec"
31 January 1785
Reproduction, original in Public Record Office

Manuscript Division, Public Archives of Canada, Ottawa

147. Padlock
Steel, held by rivets and stamped "Michel"
8.9 cm × 7.6 cm

History Division, National Museum of Man, Ottawa
No. F-590

148. Rip saw blade
Steel; wooden handles missing
137.5 cm × 8.9 cm

History Division, National Museum of Man, Ottawa
No. D-3096

149. Broad axe
Wrought iron head, steel blade, hardwood haft
Head 28.2 cm × 21.6 cm; total L. 91.4 cm

History Division, National Museum of Man, Ottawa
No. F-214

150. Carpenter's adze
Hand-forged iron head,
hand-carved wooden haft
Head 18.4 cm × 7.7 cm; total
L. 63.9 cm

History Division, National
Museum of Man, Ottawa
No. D-1667

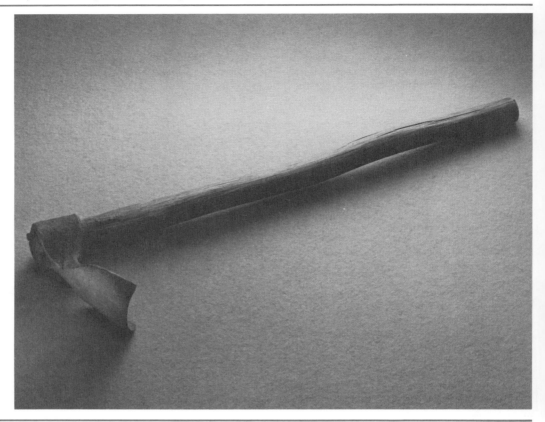

151. Hoe-type adze
Wrought iron head, wooden
haft
Head 17.5 cm × 9.3 cm; total
L. 55.5 cm
History Division, National
Museum of Man, Ottawa
No. Z-III-D-1522

152. Hoe head
Iron
15.7 cm × 8.9 cm
History Division, National
Museum of Man, Ottawa
No. X-289

153. Axe head
Iron
14.5 cm × 7.3 cm
History Division, National
Museum of Man, Ottawa
No. F-83

Loyalist Military Settlement in Upper Canada

by George A. Rawlyk

Chairman and Professor, Department of History
Queen's University, Kingston

The late-nineteenth-century mythology surrounding the Loyalist migration to what is now Ontario bears little resemblance to historical fact. Yet that myth profoundly influenced twentieth-century English-speaking Canadian values and attitudes.

A novelist and newspaperman, Loyalist William Kirby was a key articulator of this mythology:

> The war was over. Seven red years
>   of blood
> Had scourged the land from
>   mountain top to sea; . . .
> Rebellion won at last: and they
>   who loved
> The cause that had been lost, and
>   kept their faith
> To England's crown, and scorned
>   an alien name
> Passed into exile; leaving all
>   behind
> Except their honor, and the
>   conscious pride
> Of duty done to country and to
>   king.
>
> Broad lands, ancestral homes, the
>   gathered wealth
> Of patient toil and self-denying
>   years
> Were confiscated and lost; for they
>   had been
> The salt and savor of the land;
>   trained up
> In honor, loyalty, and fear of
>   God . . .
>
> Not drooping like poor fugitives,
>   they came
> In exodus to our Canadian wilds
>   . . .
> King's gifts upon the exiles were
>   bestowed.
> Ten thousand homes were
>   planted; and each one
> With axe, and fire, and mutual
>   help, made war
> Against the wilderness, and smote
>   it down . . .
> In the great woods content to
>   build a home
> And commonwealth, where they
>   could live secure
> A life of honor, loyalty, and peace.[1]

The historical evidence, however, paints a very different picture. Few of the so-called Upper-Canadian Loyalists had possessed ''broad lands, ancestral homes [and] gathered wealth'' in the Thirteen Colonies. The typical Loyalist was an illiterate subsistence farmer of German or Scots background, who had lived in one of the three northern frontier counties of New York State. He had owned or leased about one hundred acres of land and by 1776 had cleared about one-tenth of it. If foreign-born—true of about half the Loyalist population—he had arrived less than ten years before the outbreak of the American Revolution. He had served in one of the Loyalist provincial corps—Sir John Johnson's King's Royal Regiment of New York, Major Edward Jessup's Loyal Rangers, Major James Roger's King's Rangers or Lieutenant Colonel John Butler's Rangers.

The typical Upper-Canadian Loyalist was a somewhat disoriented and confused individual. By 1776 he had not as yet been totally assimilated into American society. He still tended to perceive issues and personalities within the conceptual framework of a European peasant. He retained a tenacious attachment to the land and to his ''laird'', and was deeply suspicious of change.[2] Few of these Loyalists possessed even a rudimentary grasp of the ideological underpinnings of the American Revolution. What they did understand, however, was the binding nature of an oath of allegiance and the importance of obedience and deference to authority.

''Ten thousand homes'' were not planted in the Upper-Canadian wilderness by what anti-republican Kirby and his contemporaries called ''the cream of the population of the Thirteen Colonies''. By late summer 1784 there were approximately forty-four hundred Loyalists west of the Ottawa River; by early 1786, about fifty-eight hundred. More than eighty per cent were living east of the Bay of Quinté; approximately eighteen per cent settled in the Niagara region and the remainder in and around Detroit.

In the post-revolutionary period there was another group of Loyalists residing in what is now Ontario. They were never mentioned by Kirby, and few, if any, received Lord Dorchester's ''mark of honour'' for joining ''the Royal Standard in America before the Treaty of Separation in the year 1783''.[3] These were the Iroquois, led by Joseph and Molly Brant, Loyalists who probably sacrificed far more than did their European allies for the British cause and who in fact did most of the fighting. By the end of 1785 it was estimated that more than 1800 Iroquois and their allies were living on their huge tract of superb agricultural land along the Grand River and a much smaller number on the Bay of Quinté.

Whether European or Iroquois, most of the Loyalists who eventually emigrated to Upper Canada came because in the final analysis they could not remain in or return to the United States. They did not all detest republican and democratic principles; nor were they all united in their determination to build what one of them called "the foundations of the New Empire".[4] Most of the "wretched outcasts of America", as one observer spitefully described them,[5] had come to Upper Canada to find a British asylum in what was a frontier wilderness. As American expatriates, many brought with them a sense of defeat, intense hurt, and bitter despair. But they also carried with them to Upper Canada the basic skills of frontier farming, which they had learned in northern New York, and a finely developed survival instinct.

Governor Frederick Haldimand "should ever be honored as the founder of Upper Canada".[6] The tough-minded yet sensitive Swiss soldier-administrator realized how important it was to muster, move, and settle the European Loyalists in their military units. Haldimand believed that the hard-won "mutual loyalties of comrades in war" were far too valuable to British North America "to throw away in the days of peace".[7] Those who had shared in the crucible of war, the imminence of death, and the joy of military victory deserved to be neighbours in their Loyalist "Elysium".

Eventually thirteen townships were laid out: eight Royal Townships on the St. Lawrence River and five Cataraqui Townships to the west of what is now Kingston. At the eastern extremity was Number 1 Royal Township, in which the Roman Catholic Highlanders from Sir John Johnson's Royal Regiment were settled. Next to them, in Number 2, were the Scottish Presbyterians from the same regiment, and in numbers 3, 4, and 5, German Calvinists, Lutherans, and some Anglicans. Townships 6, 7, and 8 were populated by close to five hundred men, women, and children associated with Major Jessup's Corps.

Township Number 1, Cataraqui, was allotted to a group of approximately two hundred Associated Loyalists from New York City under the leadership of Captain Michael Grass. These were refugees rather than soldiers, and were regarded by many of their Upper-Canadian neighbours, who had fought in bloody revolutionary battles, as opportunistic cowards. Township Number 2, Cataraqui, was to be home for the remainder of Jessup's Corps; and in numbers 3 and 4 were settled the 2nd Battalion of the King's Royal Regiment of New York together with Major Rogers' corps and another

group of Associated Loyalists from New York City under the command of Major Peter Van Alstyne. Number 5, farther to the southwest, was settled by a few German regulars under the command of Baron Reitzenstein, and with different detachments of disbanded Regular Regiments.[8]

Some of Butler's Rangers—fewer than three hundred families in all—were located in the Niagara region. Other members of Butler's Rangers and Loyalist officers of the British Indian Department settled in the Detroit River area, notably at Sandwich and Amherstburg.

Haldimand shaped the settlement contours of Loyalist Upper Canada in a masterly fashion, and did everything in his power to ensure that the new settlers were provided with material assistance in order to start their lives afresh.[9] He supplied the Loyalists with clothes, food, axes, hoes, spades, and seed, and provided a few sawmills and gristmills. He also determined the way in which the land would be divided. Fifty acres were to be granted to every unmarried civilian, 100 acres to the head of a family or a private soldier, and 200 acres to a noncommissioned officer. Each exsubaltern was entitled to 500 acres, each ex-captain to 700 acres, and each ex-field officer to 1000 acres. To these acreages were to be added 50 acres for each member of a settler's family.

It is interesting to note that close to ninety per cent of the Associated Loyalists and members of the King's Royal Regiment of New York actually settled on the lands set aside for them by Haldimand, but only sixty-eight per cent of Jessup's Corps and fifty-four per cent of Rogers' corps remained on their designated lands. These percentages seem to suggest that Sir John Johnson's regiment possessed the strongest social and ethnic cohesion and that the Associated Loyalists had no good reason to give up their excellent location, especially as they were not welcomed anywhere else in the region.

Recently it has been discovered that the proportion of American-born members of Jessup's and Rogers' corps was approximately three times that of Johnson's regiment. Moreover, both corps included a greater number of freehold farmers and non-farmers than did the King's Royal Regiment. Presumably these men were less deferential to those in authority than were Johnson's men, and more willing to fend for themselves in typical American frontier fashion.[10]

Despite the European Loyalists' predominantly Scotch and German background and peasant origins, some brought with them more than military experience, frontier farming skills, and a sense of defeat. A few men, who would soon become members of a small political and cultural élite, brought with them a conservative ideology or frame of mind.

Richard Cartwright, Jr., who served for a time as the military secretary to John Butler and the Rangers, is a good example of this small group of influential Loyalists. It may be argued that Cartwright was a vital link in the ideological chain that connects American Loyalist thought of the 1770s with English-speaking Tory concepts of the post-War of 1812 period. For Cartwright influenced the Reverend John Strachan—often referred to as Canada's Edmund Burke—who in turn influenced a generation of central-Canadian Tories.

Cartwright was born in Albany, New York, in 1759. In February 1777, Cartwright declared his Loyalist convictions. Despite his immaturity in many respects, he was well read in English law and history, and he had a surprisingly shrewd grasp of many of the constitutional issues involved in the revolution. He was, and would remain, an ardent advocate of the essential unity of the Anglo-American empire. And he believed that the enlightened authority and stability that emanated from King and Parliament were the only safeguards for traditional English liberties in the New World. Like other articulate members of the Loyalist élite, he perceived the republicans to be factious and anarchical, bent upon destroying both the freedoms guaranteed by the British constitution and the fragile unity of the British Empire.

On the eve of his expulsion from New York in 1777, Cartwright carefully recorded the essence of his Loyalism and that of other members of the élite, not only for that particular time, but also for the remaining years of their lives in what would become Canada. "The distracted condition of my native Country," Cartwright rather self-righteously observed, "where all Government was subverted, where Caprice was the only Rule and Measure of Usurped Authority, and where all Distress was exhibited that Power guided by Malice can produce, had long made me wish to leave it . . . notwithstanding the tender feelings of Humanity which I suffered at Parting from the fondest of Parents . . . it gave me a sensible pleasure to quit a Place where Discord reigned and all the miseries of Anarchy has long prevailed.''[11]

Like other future Loyalist leaders, Cartwright was certain that the republican demagogues had madly abandoned ''our priceless claim to all the rights and privileges of British subjects''. He saw British stability giving way to American republican anarchy. The rule of law had been overthrown by republican rule of the mob. British liberty, which guaranteed minority rights, had been cowed by Patriot intimidation, which had led to sterile conformity and worse.

Cartwright and his associates wished to transform the wilds of British North America into a prosperous and ordered ''corner of Empire''. In 1810, Cartwright wrote proudly, ''Under an Epitome of the English Constitution we enjoy the greatest practical, political Freedom.'' Many other Loyalist leaders would have soundly endorsed Cartwright's ringing declaration. They were building what they saw as a stratified, deferential, and British society, one that the distinguished New Brunswick Loyalist Edward Winslow described as possessing ''the most gentleman-like government on earth''. The Loyalist élite considered ''life, liberty and the pursuit of happiness'' to be an anarchical principle dangerous to their carefully constructed beliefs. Loyalist leaders contended that proper governments should provide guiding authority, stability, and, above all, order. The Loyalists and their successors would contrast their ideas of British order to the violence, disorder, and racism that they saw as uniquely endemic to American society.

This conservative ideology was perhaps the most important Loyalist legacy to Upper Canada, as it has profoundly affected Canadian political culture. At its core is a fascinating amalgam of psychological need and hatred for the victor—the United States.

It has been argued that the ''rigidities established by the compulsion to maintain identity'' have ''narrowed the range of political debate, channeled political thought along familiar paths, and discouraged the venturesome, the daring and the rash''.[12] Yet it may be said that the political and cultural shape of twentieth-century Ontario owes as much to the impact of the Loyalists as to any other single factor.

G.A.R.

1. Quoted in W. Kirby, *Annals of Niagara* (Toronto, 1896), pp. 81–83.

2. D.B. Rutman, *American Puritanism* (Toronto, 1977), p. 77.

3. A.L. Burt, *The Old Province of Quebec* (Toronto, 1969), vol. 2, p. 81.

4. W. Parker to C. Whitworth, 8 June 1784, PANS, MG 1, The White Collection, vol. 3, no. 283.

5. J. Bailey, quoted in A.W.H. Eaton, *The History of King's County, N.S.* (Salem, 1910), p. 107.

6. Burt, *Old Province of Quebec*, vol. 2, p. 91.

7. *Ibid.*

8. G. Craig, *Upper Canada, The Formative Years* (Toronto, 1963), p. 6.

9. Burt, *Old Province of Quebec*, vol. 2, p. 93.

10. This paragraph is based on M. Waltman's *From Soldier to Settler . . ., Patterns of Loyalist Settlement in Upper Canada, 1783–1784* (unpublished M.A. thesis, Queen's University, 1981).

11. J.J. Talman, ed., *Loyalist Narratives from Upper Canada* (Toronto, 1946), p. 45.

12. S.F. Wise and R.C. Brown, *Canada Views the United States* (Toronto, 1967), p. 96.

154. A view of the Ruins of the Fort at Cataraqui taken June 1783
James Peachey
1783
Pen and ink and watercolour on paper
37.5 cm × 57.2 cm

Picture Division, Public Archives of Canada, Ottawa
No. C-2031

In the spring of 1783, Governor Haldimand directed the surveyor general of Québec, Major Samuel Holland, to lay out townships capable of accommodating disbanded Loyalist troops and other Loyalists in the regions along the upper St. Lawrence and north shore of Lake Ontario. This view shows the Holland party at the site of the old French Fort Frontenac, the ruins of which are seen in the background. The tents of the survey party and their two-masted bateau tied up on the shore are in the middle ground.

James Peachey was a surveyor and draughtsman, as well as an accomplished artist, who began working for the Crown in Boston around 1774. He made his second voyage to North America around 1780 and returned to England in 1784. According to Samuel Holland, Peachey was ''on the footing of a Gentleman, of which he made himself deserving of, as well by his Conduct & Improvements in Drawing and Painting''. In 1787 Peachey received a commission in the 60th Foot. He died a decade later, probably during an epidemic in Martinique.

This is a rare early view of the Loyalist settlement at present-day Cornwall. There are a number of historically interesting details including the primitive structures of the Loyalists, and members of the King's Royal Regiment of New York in uniform. This was Number 1 Royal Township, which Catholic Highlanders from the King's Royal Regiment settled.

James Peachey captured this view in June 1784 while returning to Quebec from the north shore of Lake Ontario, where he had surveyed as far as Niagara.

155. Encampment of the Loyalists at Johnstown, on the banks of the River St. Lawrence in Canada
James Peachey
1785
Watercolour on paper
31.7 cm × 49.8 cm

Picture Division, Public Archives of Canada, Ottawa
No. C-2001

156. Gridiron
American
Ca. 1780
Iron; hardwood handle (later addition)
H. 17.1 cm; W. 18.4 cm

Fort Malden National Historic Park, Amherstburg, Ontario
No. F.46.94.12

157. Christine Moore's cooking pot

Early 19th century
Iron
H. 14.3 cm; Diam. 17.4 cm

Mr. Melvin Hill, Deseronto, Ontario

In 1869 Christine Moore, said to be about one hundred years old, was described as "a living relic of the American Revolution". Early in the rebellion, when she was about ten years old, she was taken captive by the Loyal Indians during an engagement with the rebels in the Mohawk Valley. She was adopted by her captors and came with them to the Bay of Quinté. Fully assimilated with her adoptive tribe, in time Christine Moore married a Mohawk named Anthony Smart.

158. The Book of Common Prayer . . . (etc.), a new edition to which is added The Gospel According to St. Mark, translated into the Mohawk Language by Captn. Joseph Brant, An Indian of the Mohawk Nation, London

1787
20.5 cm × 13.0 cm

McCord Museum, Montreal
No. RI b18.1.

Joseph Brant accomplished his translation under the auspices of the Society for the Propagation of the Gospel in Foreign Parts. Of his ability as a translator, the Reverend John Stuart said that he was "perhaps . . . the only person in America equal to such an undertaking". Brant's talents had also been valued by Sir William Johnson, who had earlier used him as an interpreter and translator of speeches. Brant spoke fluently at least three of the languages of the Six Nations.

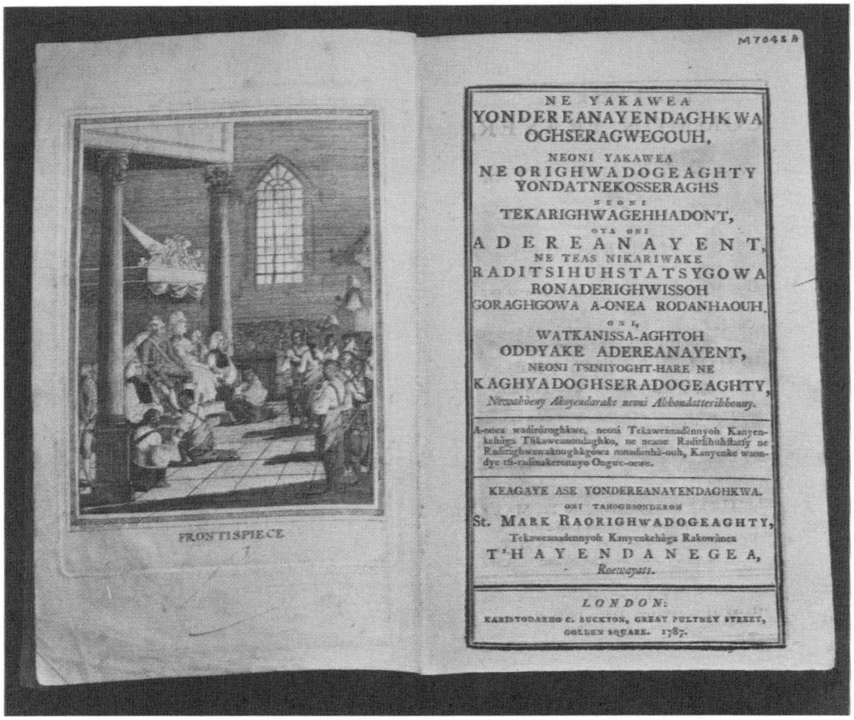

In 1770, the year of his ordination as an Anglican clergyman, John Stuart (1740–1811) was appointed missionary to the Mohawks at Fort Hunter, New York province. There he secured the collaboration of Joseph Brant in translating the Gospel of St. Mark, a concise history of the Bible, and an exposition of the catechism in the Mohawk language. During the rebellion John Stuart came to Montréal. In 1785 he became the first Anglican missionary in what became Upper Canada. At his death he was rector of St. George's Church, Kingston.

159. Reverend John Stuart
Artist Unknown
Watercolour on paper
11.9 cm × 17.7 cm

Mr. Melvin Hill, Deseronto, Ontario

A native of Stamford, Connecticut, William Jarvis (1756–1817) joined the Queen's Rangers in 1777. He served throughout the war, and was wounded at Spencer's Ordinary in June 1781 during the Virginia campaign.

After the rebellion, Jarvis went on half pay and attempted to return to Connecticut. However, the hostility towards the Loyalists was so strong that he was forced to leave. He went to England, where he secured as a patron John Graves Simcoe, the former commanding officer of the Queen's Rangers. Jarvis accompanied Simcoe to Upper Canada in 1792, and acted as provincial secretary and registrar until his death in 1817. His eldest son, Samuel Peters Jarvis (1792–1857), shown wearing an elegant reproduction of his father's uniform, served in the War of 1812. During the Rebellion of 1837, he was instrumental in briefly reconstituting the Queen's Rangers.

160. Mr. Secretary Jarvis with his son Samuel Peters Jarvis
Attributed to Matthew William Peters
English
Ca. 1791
Oil on canvas
104.1 cm × 86.4 cm

Royal Ontario Museum, Toronto
Purchased with the assistance of a Canadian Cultural Property Grant
No. 981.79.1

161. Hannah Jarvis with her daughters, Maria Lavinia and Augusta Honoria

Attributed to Matthew William Peters
English
Ca. 1791
Oil on canvas
104.1 cm × 86.4 cm

Royal Ontario Museum, Toronto
Purchased with the assistance of a Canadian Cultural Property Grant
No. 981.79.2

Hannah Owen Peters was the daughter of Reverend Samuel Peters of Hebron, Connecticut. She married William Jarvis in 1785 in St. George's Church, Hanover Square, London. They had three sons and four daughters.

162. Walking stick of Simon Girty

Wood
L. 84.0 cm

Fort Malden National Historic Park, Amherstburg, Ontario
No. F.41.151.15

A native of Pennsylvania, Simon Girty (1741–1818) joined the British Indian Department at the outbreak of the rebellion and assisted the Indians of the Ohio country in holding back the American rebels. After the conflict, Girty and several of his colleagues in the Indian department, including Matthew Elliott and Alexander McKee, continued to support the tribes. Girty eventually acquired land and settled along the Detroit River near Amherstburg.

Matthew Elliott (1739–1814) was an Irishman who settled in Pennsylvania in 1761. He was an Indian fighter at the Pontiac uprising, a fur trader, an Indian emissary, and an officer in the British Indian Department. After the rebellion, he settled near Amherstburg, and was elected three times to the Legislative Assembly of Upper Canada. He continued his work with the Indian department in Upper Canada, and by 1808 was considered the "only man capable of calling forth the loyalties of the Indians". Appointed superintendent of Indian affairs at Fort Malden (Amherstburg), he served throughout the War of 1812.

163. Coatee of Matthew Elliott
Ca. 1812
Wool, scarlet with blue facings

Fort Malden National Historic Park, Amherstburg, Ontario
No. FF 75.8.2

164. Peter Drummond's Commission as Captain, Royal Canadian Volunteers
1795
Parchment
33.0 cm × 29.0 cm

Canadian War Museum, Ottawa
No. 1982-550/9

During the rebellion Peter Drummond rose to the rank of captain with Colonel Edward Jessup's Loyal Rangers. He later settled in Edwardsburg Township, Grenville County.

Following the outbreak of war between Great Britain and Revolutionary France in 1793, Lord Dorchester raised the Royal Canadian Volunteers. There were two battalions, one French speaking, the other English speaking. Together they constituted a regiment of colonial regulars.

The Loyalist Tradition
by Ann Gorman Condon

The history of the Loyalists is a subtle combination of fact, remembered fact, and myth. The actual experience of these people—Revolutionary war, exile, and resettlement—is most important. But Loyalist history includes as well memories of Loyalist settlers and veterans, stories told to children and grandchildren, legends, heroic tales, and emotional associations that grew up around the actual events. These are collectively known as "the Loyalist tradition". In Canada, Loyalist social and political values remained a vital force throughout the nineteenth century; and the tradition was most influential between the Loyalist centennial celebrations of 1883–1884 and the outbreak of the First World War. Most supporters of this tradition were direct descendants, but many other Canadians adopted the viewpoint and principles of the Loyalists. Different elements in the tradition would be stressed at different times, according to the needs of the moment.

The most famous characteristic of the Loyalist tradition is, of course, loyalty to the Crown. The Loyalists and their descendants were not alone in this sentiment: virtually all Canadians in the nineteenth century recognized that their survival depended directly on British protection, and they deeply valued the self-government granted them under the British constitution. However, the Loyalists and their descendants regarded themselves as the special defenders of the British connection, the North American guardians of British culture and British manners.

On public anniversaries, the Loyalist vow to "Fear God and Honour the King" would be reaffirmed and tales of Loyalist sacrifices retold.[1] Torchlight parades, political oratory, fireworks, religious sermons, and patriotic odes reminded the public of the link between the loyal colonies and the mother country. Unable to serve their monarch directly, Loyalists dominated the various militia units. The men exhibited their ardour by donning elaborate uniforms, menacing sabres, and plumed helmets; the ladies celebrated their patriotism by wearing ball gowns patterned after the Union Jack and headdresses incorporating imperial motifs. Those who could travelled frequently to England, sent their sons to English schools, and entertained in the grand Victorian manner so effectively described in Mazo de la Roche's saga of Jalna. For these Loyalist descendants, the imperial tie redeemed Canadian society from the brash materialism of the New World and made it part of a powerful, civilized, international community.

The pride and self-awareness that Loyalist adherents derived from the British connection slowly evolved into a sense of Canadian nationalism after Confederation in 1867. In the 1870s Loyalist descendants spearheaded the Canada First Movement, a gentlemen's literary group committed to publicizing the virtues of their "new northern nation".[2] The Loyalist centennial celebrations of 1883–1884 provoked even more exuberant expressions of national pride and imperial sentiment, particularly in Toronto and Saint John. The United Empire Loyalists' Association of Canada, the New Brunswick Historical Society, and the International Order of the Daughters of the Empire were established at this time, and began the important work of preserving and publishing the documents of their Loyalist ancestors. The final manifestation was the Imperial Federation Movement, which glorified the empire, the Anglo-Saxon race, and the Canadian nation. However, its sentiments were unacceptable to many Canadians. As controversy arose over participation in the Boer War and First World War, the influence of the Loyalist tradition on Canadian public life effectively ended.

The pro-British bias of the Loyalist tradition naturally included a virulent anti-Americanism. The Loyalists' deep-rooted hostility towards the United States was well expressed in Edward Winslow's vow that the new province of New Brunswick would become "the envy of the American states".[3] The memory of military defeat and loss, continuing resentment about the great growth and prosperity of the new republic, and a genuine fear of American expansionism ensured that this hostility and distrust would continue to be a powerful force in Canadian history. It comforted Canadians to feel that theirs was a morally superior society, and newspapers entertained their readers with a steady stream of reports on the more lurid aspects of southern slavery, lynching parties, urban crime, and machine politics. However, the republic's excesses did not deter the Loyalists and their descendants from paying long, affectionate visits to their relatives in the "Boston States" or from seeking employment in the New England mills and the great urban centres of the Midwest or from going "all the way west to Bangor" to outfit the family for winter.

In addition to implanting deep within Canadian cultural attitudes an affection for Great Britain and resentment towards the United States, the Loyalist legacy has profoundly influenced the development and government of the Canadian people. Four beliefs and practices are of special significance: the Loyalist military tradition, the Loyalist élite's concept of oligarchic government, the Loyalist preference for democratic forms of government and religion, and, finally, Loyalist proposals for a federal union of Britain's colonies in North America.

The Loyalist military tradition did not end with the Revolutionary War. When the provincial regiments moved north, they brought with them their memories, their *esprit de corps* and their readiness to take up arms in defence of the Crown. Many Loyalists joined local militia units or provincial fencible regiments. A number recorded their wartime experiences in personal memoirs or in petitions submitted to the Loyalist Claims Commission to get compensation for their suffering and losses. These activities and records provided the foundation for an indigenous military tradition in Canada.

The War of 1812 provided a glorious counterpoint to the defeat of 1783. In both the Maritimes and the Canadas, the thrill of seeing Great Britain give the Americans ''the chastisement which they so richly deserve''[4] was a source of satisfaction to many Loyalist veterans like Edward Winslow. But the war had a second, more profound impact. In Upper Canada particularly, it forced the question of allegiance which hung over many of that province's ''late Loyalist'' and recent American immigrants. General Isaac Brock's victories at Detroit and Queenston Heights convinced these recent arrivals that Great Britain was determined to defend her colonies in North America. If they wanted to remain in British territory, they had to declare their allegiance to the Crown. In a very real sense, the War of 1812 guaranteed the integrity and permanence of the young colonies in British North America, and many historians date the beginnings of Canadian nationalism from its outcome.

As the Loyalist military traditions evolved during the nineteenth century, the loyal settlers of Upper Canada were given the greatest credit for the defence of their homeland, even though professional historians report that British troops bore the brunt of the fighting. This discrepancy points up the distinction between fact and tradition: the Loyalist contribution to the war effort was mythologized into heroic proportions to provide Upper Canada with a glorious military past that would enable its inhabitants to build on a common bond of sacrifice, courage, and commitment.

Second only to their military tradition, the Loyalists are renowned for their concept of élite leadership. Although modern historians have considerably qualified earlier accounts of Loyalist grandeur, it remains that the Loyalists introduced an aristocratic principle into the government and culture of the original provinces of British North America. Their goal was to establish a hierarchical society, in which power and responsibility would flow from the top down—from the king to his governor, on to the appointed council and judges, and finally down to the elected assembly where a limited power would serve popular needs. The élite set its power base on three key institutions: a ruling oligarchy of appointed officials holding most of the political power; an established church that would inculcate loyalty and respect for the established order; and a sophisticated propertied class that the oligarchy would recruit into public service by special land grants and other favours of government.

While government from above proved effective in getting the Loyalists resettled and in establishing new community institutions, its long-term prospects in British North America were poor, as the rebellions and reform movements of the 1830s proved. Joseph Howe would dismiss the élite rulers of Nova Scotia as government by ''twelve old ladies''. The ''necromancy'' of New Brunswick,[5] the Chateau Clique of Lower Canada,[6] and the Family Compact of Upper Canada[7] failed to win the support of the majority of the people.

During their brief tenure in power, however, the Loyalist élite made substantial contributions to Canadian life. They believed firmly in the ability of government to create a strong, harmonious society. They established in the frontier settlements a stable legal system based on ancient British principles. They gave official encouragement to the Anglican Church and set up universities and grammar schools that endure to this day. They brought an element of learning and refinement to an otherwise uncultivated society and left a heritage of fine houses, elegant furnishings, and sophisticated style. Finally, out of their American experience came an understanding of the need for a policy of tolerance towards religious dissenters and ethnic minorities, which laid the basis for Canada's distinctive social outlook. Long after the Loyalists disappeared as a governing class, their conservative philosophy and many of their descendants continued "to find places of honour and status for themselves".

Directly contradicting the élite's determination to set up a privileged ruling class is the third element in the Loyalist tradition—its democratic thrust. The vast majority of the Loyalists were, of course, farmers, fishermen, pioneers, small tradesmen. They were certainly loyal but their years in the American colonies had accustomed them to local government, to participating in public debate, and to choosing their own political representatives. When they resettled in British North America after the revolution, they brought these democratic expectations with them—they were not republicans, but democracy was bred in their bones.

This egalitarian impulse had profound implications for Canada's political and social history. In politics it was reinforced by the democratic wave of the land-hungry British immigrants who poured into British North America after the War of 1812, and of the upstart American pioneers who brought to Upper Canada the heady populism of Jacksonian Democracy. Outraged by the privileges of the Loyalist élite, these democratic forces dismantled the old provincial hierarchies and placed in their stead Canada's distinctive form of parliamentary democracy—responsible government. In this struggle, such Loyalist tribunes as Elias Hardy and Joseph Howe deserve credit alongside Louis-Joseph Papineau, William Lyon Mackenzie, and Robert Baldwin.

The democratic element within the Loyalist movement could also be seen in religious matters. Notwithstanding their demonstrated allegiance to the British Crown, most Loyalists were not members of the Church of England. Some belonged to other well-established churches, mainly the Presbyterian and Roman Catholic. But an enormous number of these settlers, living fragile, isolated lives in the wilderness, found attractive what Bishop Charles Inglis called the "Fanaticks"—the Baptists, Methodists, and other itinerant sects.[8] These groups fiercely resented the wealth and privilege of the Anglican church, particularly its control of higher education. Their unflagging efforts to destroy such privilege brought the evangelical Protestant sects into public life and produced Tory radicalism. Egerton Ryerson, son of a Loyalist and a Methodist minister, combined a fervent devotion to the monarchy with an intense sense of religious duty towards the humbler members of society. While Ryerson was busy establishing the public-school system in Upper Canada, like-minded groups of Methodists and Baptists were founding Mount Allison and Acadia universities in the Maritimes. This commitment of Tory radicalism to human equality and social betterment would continue to shape Canadian social policy in profound ways.

Thus the Loyalists brought with them two political traditions: oligarchy, government by an élite, and democracy, government by the people. The clashes between these two principles kept colonial politics in turmoil throughout the colonial period. Yet the creative tension between élitist and democratic traditions in the Canadian body politic gave the new society added depth and complexity. Canada is surely richer today because she possesses, in addition to the modern democratic ethos, historic customs that foster a well-trained public service, dignified rituals, and high cultural style.

The fourth significant element in the Loyalist tradition is a preference for a federation of all the British provinces under one government. As early as 1754, certain colonial Americans were calling for a union of the Thirteen Colonies into a single political unit that would govern itself internally and deal on a collective basis with the imperial authorities. Led at first by Benjamin Franklin, this group promoted an Anglo-American union, and attracted many Loyalists—notably William Smith, Jr., and Joseph Galloway—who viewed the scheme as a workable alternative to revolution. After the Revolutionary War, such Loyalists as Jonathan Sewell and William Smith urged the imperial government to organize the remaining British provinces into a political federation. These proposals fell by the wayside, but the idea of a federation within the British empire was kept alive by two Loyalist sons, Jonathan Sewell, Jr., Chief Justice of Lower Canada, and Thomas Chandler Haliburton, Supreme Court Justice of Nova Scotia.

In 1839 Sewell found a receptive audience in Lord Durham, who reviewed the old Loyalist plans and cited them in his famous report to demonstrate the historical basis for a union of the Canadian provinces. While these Loyalist plans were only one element of Durham's recommendations and the subsequent confederation of the provinces in 1867, they do establish the Loyalists as early advocates of dominion status: a self-governing union of free people within the British family of nations.

How should we evaluate the contribution of the Loyalists as we commemorate their bicentennial? There is no doubt that the loyal Americans made a formative contribution to national development—they helped weave the basic political and cultural fabric of the evolving dominion. Like the French Canadians, the Loyalists overcame defeat to build a new, vibrant society that embodied their ideals; and Canadians continue to reap the benefits of their belief in free political institutions and human dignity. The Loyalist bicentennial offers both Canadians and Americans an opportunity to examine afresh the rich legacy left by the loyal Americans. Exploring the essential elements of the Loyalist tradition is a means of gaining a better understanding and appreciation of ourselves.

A.G.C.

1. E.C. Wright, *The Loyalists of New Brunswick* (Fredericton, 1955), pp. 1–2.
2. C. Berger, *The Sense of Power: Studies in the Ideas of Canadian Imperialism, 1867–1914* (Toronto, 1970), pp. 49–77.
3. W.O. Raymond, ed., *The Winslow Papers* (Saint John, 1901), p. 193.
4. *Ibid.*, p. 669.
5. E. Winslow to Governor T. Carleton, 31 November 1805, University of New Brunswick Archives, Winslow Family Papers.
6. M. Wade, *The French Canadians, 1760–1967* (Toronto, 1968), p. 104*f.*
7. D.W.L. Earl, ed., *The Family Compact: Aristocracy or Oligarchy?* (Toronto, 1967), *passim.*
8. W.S. McNutt, *The Atlantic Provinces: The Emergence of a Colonial Society* (Toronto, 1972), pp. 160–62.

165. Loyalist Centennial Souvenir
New Brunswick Historical Society, Saint John
1887
14.7 cm × 20.4 cm

New Brunswick Museum, Saint John

This publication was produced by the New Brunswick Historical Society (founded in 1874) to celebrate the one-hundredth anniversary of the landing of the Loyalists in New Brunswick.

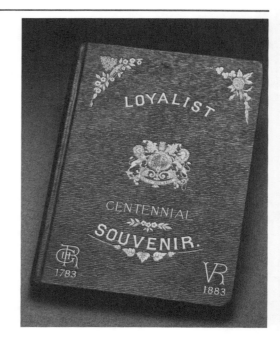

166. Medal commemorating the unveiling of the Brant Memorial at Brantford, Ontario
Struck by P.W. Ellis & Co., Toronto
1886
Bronze
Obverse, bust of Joseph Brant
Diam. 3.8 cm

National Medal Collection, Public Archives of Canada, Ottawa
No. 1924

**167. Medal
commemorating the
unveiling of the
Brant Memorial at
Brantford, Ontario**
Struck by P.W. Ellis & Co.,
Toronto
1886
White metal
Reverse, representation of the
Brant Memorial
Diam. 3.8 cm

National Medal Collection,
Public Archives of Canada,
Ottawa
No. 1925

The Great Seal of the new Loyalist province arrived from England in 1785. The obverse portrays a forested settlement along the bank of a river. On the water rides a three-masted vessel with sails unfurled. Beneath this scene is the provincial motto *Spem reduxit* ("It restored hope"), which refers to the new hope of the Loyalists who came to New Brunswick following the rebellion.

**168. Seal of the Province
of New Brunswick**
New Brunswick
Wax
Obverse
Diam. 11.2 cm

New Brunswick Museum, Saint
John
No. 29941

This document concerns property in the parish of Newcastle, Northumberland County, New Brunswick. The reverse of the Seal of the Province bears the Royal Arms of George III.

**169. Land grant with
attached map and seal**
New Brunswick
1810
Document of paper, seal of wax
Reverse of seal
Document, 54.5 cm × 37.5 cm;
seal diam. 11.2 cm

New Brunswick Museum, Saint
John

170. United Empire Loyalist celebration
Ontario
1929
Photograph
96.7 cm × 18.8 cm

Mr. Melvin Hill, Deseronto,
Ontario

171. Loyalist commemorative plate
Wood and Sons, Burslem,
Staffordshire
Ca. 1930
English white earthenware with
transfer print
Diam. 25.5 cm

Canadian War Museum, Ottawa
No. 1981-217/1

172. Loyalist settler's cabin, Upper Canada Village, Ontario
Harry Foster photograph
1982
90.0 cm × 60.0 cm

National Museum of Man,
Ottawa

Bibliography

Sources

Cruikshank, E.A., ed. *The Settlement of the United Empire Loyalists on the Upper St. Lawrence and Bay of Quinte in 1784: a Documentary Record*. Toronto: Ontario Historical Society, 1934.

Johnston, J.K., ed. *The Valley of the Six Nations: A Collection of Documents on the Indian Lands of the Grand River*. Toronto: Champlain Society, 1964.

Palmer, G., ed. *A Bibliography of Loyalist Source Material in the United States, Canada, and Great Britain*. Westport, Conn. and London: Meckler Publishing in association with the American Antiquarian Society, 1982.

Preston, R.A., ed. *Kingston before the War of 1812: A Collection of Documents*. Toronto: Champlain Society, 1959.

Raymond, W.O., ed. *The Winslow Papers, A.D. 1776–1836*. Saint John: New Brunswick Historical Society Collections, 1901; reprinted, Boston: Gregg Press, 1972.

Simcoe, Lt. Col. J.G., *Simcoe's Military Journal: A History of the Operations of a Partisan Corps Called the Queen's Rangers*. New York, 1844; reprinted, Toronto: Baxter Publishing, 1962.

Talman, J.J., ed. *Loyalist Narratives from Upper Canada*. Toronto: Champlain Society, 1946.

Studies

Allen, R.S. *Loyalist Literature: An Annotated Bibliographic Guide to the Writings on the Loyalists of the American Revolution*. Toronto: Dundurn Press, 1982.

Archibald, M. *Gideon White, Loyalist*. Halifax: published with the assistance of the Nova Scotia Museum, 1975.

Blakeley, P.R. and Grant, G., eds. *Eleven Exiles: Accounts of Loyalists of the American Revolution*. Toronto: Dundurn Press, 1982.

Brown, W. *The Good Americans: The Loyalists in the American Revolution*. New York: Wm. Morrow, 1969; and *The King's Friends: The Composition and Motives of the American Loyalist Claimants*. Providence, R.I.: Brown University Press, 1965.

Calhoon, R.M. *The Loyalists in Revolutionary America, 1760–1781*. New York: Harcourt Brace Jovanovich, 1973.

Cruikshank, E.A. *Butler's Rangers: The Revolutionary Period*. Welland, Ont., 1893; reprinted, Owen Sound, 1975.

Duffy, D. *Gardens, Covenants, Exiles: Loyalism in the Literature of Upper Canada/Ontario*. Toronto: University of Toronto Press, 1982.

Finley, A.G. *The Loyalists*. Saint John: New Brunswick Museum, [1975].

Flowers, A.D. *The Loyalists of Bay Chaleur*. Victoria: private printing, 1973.

Fryer, M.B. *King's Men: the Soldier-Founders of Ontario*. Toronto: Dundurn Press, 1980.

Gilroy, M. *Loyalists and Land Settlement in Nova Scotia*. Halifax: Public Archives of Nova Scotia, publication no. 4, 1937; reprinted, Royal Nova Scotia Historical Society (with index), 1975.

Graymont, B. *The Iroquois in the American Revolution*. Syracuse: Syracuse University Press, 1972.

Hill, I.L. *Some Loyalists and Others*. Fredericton: private printing, 1976.

Katcher, P. *The American Provincial Corps, 1775–1784*. Reading, England: Osprey Publishing, 1973.

Mathews, H.C. *The Mark of Honour*. Toronto: University of Toronto Press, 1965.

Nelson, W.H. *The American Tory*. Oxford: Clarendon Press, 1961.

Norton, M.B. *The British-Americans; The Loyalist Exiles in England, 1774–1789*. Boston and Toronto: Little, Brown, 1972.

Roberts, K. *Oliver Wiswell*. New York: Doubleday, Doran, 1940.

Robertson, M. *A History of Early Shelburne: Founded in 1783 by the Port Roseway Associates, Loyalists of the American Revolution*. Halifax: Nova Scotia Museum, (n.d.).

Smith, P.H. *Loyalists and Redcoats: A Study in British Revolutionary Policy*. New York: W.W. Norton, 1972.

Smy, Lt. Col. W.A. *Rolls of the Provincial Loyalist Corps, Canadian Command American Revolutionary War*. Toronto: Dundurn Press, 1981.

Stryker, W.S. *The New Jersey Volunteers, Loyalists*. Trenton, N.J., 1887.

Troxler, C.W. *The Migration of Carolina and Georgia Loyalists to Nova Scotia and New Brunswick*. Unpublished Ph.D. thesis, University of North Carolina, 1974.

Upton, L.F.S., ed. *The United Empire Loyalists: Men and Myths*. Toronto: Copp Clark, 1967.

Walker, J.W. St. G. *The Black Loyalists: The Search for a Promised Land in Nova Scotia and Sierra Leone, 1783–1870*. New York and Halifax: Africana Publishing with Dalhousie University Press, 1976.

Wilson, B. *As She Began: An Illustrated Introduction to Loyalist Ontario*. Toronto: Dundurn Press, 1981.

Wright, E.C. *The Loyalists of New Brunswick*. Fredericton: private printing, 1975.

Articles

Barkley, M. "The Loyalist Tradition in New Brunswick: The Growth and Evolution of an Historical Myth, 1825–1914." *Acadiensis*, vol. 4 (1975), pp. 3–45.

Berger, C. "The Loyalist Tradition." *The Sense of Power: Studies in the Ideas of Canadian Imperialism, 1867–1914*. Toronto: University of Toronto Press, 1970.

Christie, I.R. "The Imperial Dimension: British Ministerial Perspective during the American Revolutionary Crisis, 1763–1776." *Red, White and True Blue: The Loyalists in the American Revolution*, edited by E. Wright. New York: AMS Press, 1976.

Cruikshank, E.A. "The Coming of the Loyalist Mohawks to the Bay of Quinte." *Ontario Historical Society Papers and Records*, vol. 26 (1930), pp. 390–403; and "The King's Royal Regiment of New York." *Ibid.*, vol. 27 (1931), pp. 1–131.

Ells, M. "Loyalist Attitudes." *Dalhousie Review*, vol. 15 (1935), pp. 320–34; and "Settling the Loyalists in Nova Scotia." *Canadian Historical Association Report for 1934*, pp. 105–9.

Fellows, R. "The Loyalists and Land Settlement in New Brunswick, 1783–90." *The Canadian Archivist*, vol. 2 (1970), pp. 5–15.

Gilliam, F.E. "The Loyalists in Prince Edward Island." *Royal Society of Canada, Proceedings and Transactions*, 3rd series, vol. 4 (1910), pp. 109–17.

Lampee, T.C. "The Missisquoi Loyalists." *Proceedings of the Vermont Historical Society*, vol. 6 (1938), pp. 81–140.

Longley, R.C. "An Annapolis County Loyalist." *Collections of the Nova Scotia Historical Society*, vol. 31 (1957), pp. 73–95; and "The DeLancey Brothers, Loyalists of Annapolis County." *Ibid.*, vol. 32 (1958), pp. 55–77.

MacKinnon, N. "Nova Scotia Loyalists, 1783–1785." *Social History*, no. 4 (1969), pp. 17–48.

Morgan, R.J. "The Loyalists of Cape Breton." *Dalhousie Review*, vol. 55 (1975), pp. 5–22.

Raddall, T.H. "Tarleton's Legion." *Collections of the Nova Scotia Historical Society*, vol. 28 (1947), pp. 1–50.

Raymond, W.O. "The Founding of Shelburne: Benjamin Marston at Halifax, Shelburne and Miramichi." *Collections of the New Brunswick Historical Society*, no. 8 (1909), pp. 204–7; and "Loyalists in Arms." *Ibid.*, no. 5 (1904), pp. 189–223.

Senior, E. "Loyalist Regiments after the American Revolution." *Canadian Genealogist*, vol. 2 (1980), pp. 31–46.

Shelton, W.G. "The United Empire Loyalists: A Reconsideration." *Dalhousie Review*, vol. 45 (1965), pp. 5–16.

Siebert, W.H. "The American Loyalists in the Eastern Seigniories and Townships of Province of Quebec." *Royal Society of Canada, Proceedings and Transactions*, 3rd series, vol. 7 (1914), section 2, pp. 3–4; and "The Exodus of the Loyalists from Penobscot and the Loyalist Settlements at Passamaquoddy." *Collections of the New Brunswick Historical Society*, vol. 9 (1914), pp. 485–529.

Smith, T.W. "The Loyalists at Shelburne." *Collections of the Nova Scotia Historical Society*, vol. 6 (1888), pp. 53–89.

Stuart, E.R. "Jessup's Rangers as a Factor in Loyalist Settlement." *Three History Theses*. Toronto: Ontario Department of Public Records and Archives, 1961.

Torok, C.H. "The Tyendinaga Mohawks." *Ontario History*, vol. 57 (1965), pp. 69–77.

Wise, S.F. "Upper Canada and the Conservative Tradition." *Profiles of a Province: Studies in the History of Ontario*, edited by J.J. Talman. Toronto: Ontario Historical Society, 1967, pp. 20–33.

Contributors

The Canadian War Museum gratefully acknowledges the contributions of the following major lenders to *The Loyal Americans:*

The New Brunswick Museum, Saint John, New Brunswick

Mr. Warren Moore, Greensboro, North Carolina

The Public Archives of Canada, Ottawa, Ontario

Mr. John Wentworth Moody, Ottawa, Ontario

The McCord Museum, Montréal, Québec

The National Museum of Man, History Division, Ottawa, Ontario

University of King's College, Halifax, Nova Scotia

The Royal Ontario Museum, Toronto, Ontario

Fort Malden National Historic Park, Amherstburg, Ontario

Mr. Melvin Hill, Deseronto, Ontario

The Public Archives of Nova Scotia, Halifax, Nova Scotia

Bayerisches Armeemuseum, Ingolstadt, Federal German Republic

Mr. and Mrs. George Bruce, Shelburne, Nova Scotia

The following individuals and institutions have generously contributed single works to the exhibition:

Mr. Robert Adams, Burlington, Ontario

The Beaverbrook Art Gallery, Fredericton, New Brunswick

The Anne S.K. Brown Military Collection, Providence, Rhode Island

Mr. Harold Denton, Digby, Nova Scotia

Fort George National Historic Park, Niagara-on-the-Lake, Ontario

Mr. George DeLancey Hanger, Roanoke, Virginia

King's Landing Historical Settlement, Fredericton, New Brunswick

The Nor'Wester and Loyalist Museum, Williamstown, Ontario

The Macdonald-Stewart Foundation, Montréal, Québec

Dr. D.R. MacInnis, Shubenacadie, Nova Scotia

The Lord Maclean, London, England

The Earl and Countess of Malmesbury, Basingstoke, Hants, England

The Metropolitan Museum of Art, New York, New York

Le Musée de l'île Sainte-Hélène, Montréal, Québec

Le Musée du Québec, Québec, Québec

The National Gallery of Canada, Ottawa, Ontario

Staatliche Graphische Sammlung, Munich, Federal German Republic

Toronto Historical Board, Old Fort York, Toronto, Ontario

Mr. Harold Trask, Nepean, Ontario

Mr. Lister Fanning Trask, Digby, Nova Scotia

Mrs. H.H. Winter, Ottawa, Ontario

Mr. Victor Zabatiuk, Cornwall, Ontario

Index